This book is a gift from

_____

to

_____

because I care about you.

"NOT ME!"

SECOND EDITION

Important New Information

Recognize DANGER
AND RESPOND Safely

AL HORNER

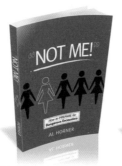

OTHER BOOKS BY AL HORNER

Studies related to assaults are many and as varied as are the conclusions reached in those studies. The statistics suggested in this book are approximations derived from the review of many studies. Proper responses to threats are many and varied, and experts sometimes disagree about best practices. The actions suggested in this book are consensus opinions of experienced people, but the suggested actions should not be construed as always correct. Each dangerous situation is unique, and the situation must dictate the action by the person being threatened. There are no absolute right actions for all situations. Only the person being threatened can properly decide what action should be taken at any particular time or in any particular situation. Neither the author, the publisher, nor Not Me! trainers shall be liable or responsible for any loss, injury, or damage allegedly arising from any information or suggestion in this book. The person who is in danger is solely responsible for his/her actions. All matters related to the legality of actions in response to threats should be discussed with an attorney licensed to practice in your area.

Table of Contents

Acknowledgments

Diane Horner has been trying to educate me for almost fifty years. She is the most powerful influence in my life and is the lead instructor in my lessons-learned about the realities of women's lives. Words can't describe how much I value her.

Karla Rapp has been the second most influential person in the evolution of Not Me! Her fingerprints are all over what we do and she has guided me toward clearer understanding of a woman's perspectives on many issues. Thank you, Karla.

Diane Dunning, Alison James, Kassandra Moore, Kathryn Carlson, Brooke Aulik, Shanna Hanson, Barbara Everett, and Cara Bishop have all influenced what we do and how we do it. Each has been an important part of our growth process. Thank you for your involvement and support.

Carrie Donovan, you remain an inspiration for all who know your story. You are a special person. On behalf of all the women who are inspired by your strength and courage, "Thank you."

Pat Fallon, you started all this by trusting me to help your daughter. Thank you for being the first supporter.

To all the women who have attended our classes and told your stories, thank you for having the courage to discuss those events. Your strength and willingness to share has provided information that prevents pain and saves lives every time we teach a class and every time someone reads this book.

The team at Koechel Peterson Design has shaped how we look in this book. If you find the appearance of this book appealing, they did it. Thank you to David Koechel, Gregory Rohm and Lance Wubbels for capturing our message in four-color images.

introduction

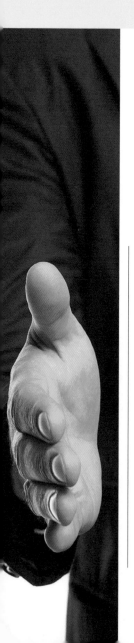

Introduction

It all started when a friend asked me to find a class that would help his college-bound daughter be safer. I found several self-defense classes, but all were taught by people with martial arts or law enforcement backgrounds. The first group focused on physical moves to defeat attackers and the second on rules to avoid danger. Neither approach dealt adequately with the breadth and complexity of realities young women face in the real world. I told my friend about my concern. He asked if I would put together a class. I agreed to do it.

She and her friends liked what I taught them. They told others, and they told others. Class followed class. As I taught, I began to realize how much I didn't know. My education began.

As a Navy SEAL officer, I felt empowered and was not afraid of much. The women in our classes opened my eyes to a world that was shockingly different than mine. For example, I normally walk to my car after dark thinking about what I've just done or what I'll do tomorrow. Women focus on whether there are any men in the dark parking lot. I am free to let my mind wander; they have to live here and now. During my days, I don't worry about someone getting aggressive with me—I will handle it. Women must be alert to threats, remembering stories of assaulted women and the consequences in their lives. My world has few of the concerns that women deal with continuously. I just don't get it about a woman's world. Most men don't.

Teachers started appearing. My wife, Diane, was the first, saying something like, "You are a 6'2", 220-pound male who was a SEAL. I am 5'3", 105-pound dancer. I must do things differently than you, because your approach won't work for me." Another Diane, who had been the victim in a horrible assault, helped me understand how a strong woman can be terribly violated and survive. The teachers continued: Karla, Krista, Suzanne, Carol, Kat, Kassie, Ali, Cara, and many other wonderful women who guided this Neanderthal through a world of new issues and feelings.

Our classes grew. Over 10,000 girls and women have participated. The number of stories we have heard grows. And what we teach in our classes evolves in response to what our team learns from women who have faced danger and won.

I'll never fully understand a woman's world. But I am blessed by close association with bright, strong women who are passionate about women's safety for a variety of very personal reasons and are willing to continually educate me. In combination we are 1 + 1 = 3, each of us helping the other be more than we can be alone.

My first book, "*Not Me!*" was well received. This book is a more powerful treatment of the most important topics. We discuss serious issues, but our class participants say they feel empowered like never before. Enjoy this experience and be safer.

Al Horner

chapter **1**

Understanding
What's Real

chapter 1
Understanding **What's Real**

The bad news: Our world can be dangerous. The good news: You can take control of your environment and be safer.

Many of us live in a bubble of denial. It's not fun to think about living in a world where bad stuff happens. Often we pretend it doesn't exist or we turn our backs when the facts get tough. If you are willing to burst the bubble of denial, you and those you care about will live more safely. Consider this: 70% of Earth is covered by water. It is wise to learn how to swim so you can save yourself if you need to. Consider this: 1 of 4 women in the U.S. will face a sexual assault in her lifetime. It is wise to learn how to manage danger. We will show you how.

INFORMATION LEADS TO BELIEFS; BELIEFS LEAD TO ACTIONS
"If you don't fight, you won't get hurt so badly—maybe he won't kill you." That belief was common not so long ago and still lingers as truth for many. Diane and her friends were among those believers. When she was assaulted by a stranger,

she complied, believing that was the wise choice. When the attack became really bad, she shut down and went numb, letting the attacker do what he wanted. As a result, she was brutally raped. The negative consequences of that assault have affected her throughout her life.

Diane's information was wrong. Current studies and information are clear—strong resistance to an attack leads to better outcomes than compliance. Department of Justice surveys indicate about 85% of victims who resisted believe their resistance produced a better outcome than not resisting would have. Emergency room professionals say the same thing.

An emergency room doctor from a major hospital brought his daughter to a Not Me! class and shared his personal experience. When assault victims come into his emergency room, those who resisted and stopped the assault typically have unsubstantial injuries, such as bumps, bruises, and cuts. Those who did not resist and let the attacker do what he wanted typically have much more serious injuries—injuries so serious he didn't want to describe them in front of his daughter and her friends.

If your information consists of "Don't fight and you won't get hurt so badly," and you believe it, your reaction to an attacker will be submission. That outdated information has produced an immense amount of unnecessary pain.

Information leads to beliefs; beliefs lead to actions. We are about to provide you pieces of information. The numbers we quote are estimates. Victims are typically reluctant to report or discuss their assaults—completely understandable—so even the most disciplined data collection efforts have caveats about the precision of their numbers. Our numbers are compilations of information we have collected from:

- Department of Justice data tables
- Research studies
- Feedback from 10,000+ class participants
- Personal experience

If you choose to believe this information, you will automatically take actions that will keep you safer.

WHO, WHAT, WHEN, WHERE, AND HOW

Who gets attacked? Out of 10 women, how many are likely to face an attempted sexual assault in their lifetime?

About 25%. Minority women and women in lower economic groups are at increased risk. Their numbers are closer to 33%.

1 in 4 Females Will Face an Attack in Her Lifetime

60% of sexual assaults are not reported to police

Which age groups face the most attempted assaults?

About 50% of assaults occur between ages 13 and 24—that is the peak assault period. About 80% of assaults occur before age 34. Though the frequency of assaults reaches a peak as young women begin doing things independently, the threat of assault never ends. Emergency rooms often see senior women who have been raped.

Young Women are at the Greatest Risk.

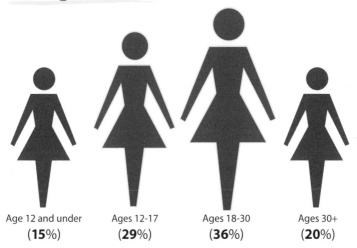

| Age 12 and under | Ages 12-17 | Ages 18-30 | Ages 30+ |
| **(15**%) | **(29**%) | **(36**%) | **(20**%) |

Who attacks?

Rank in order from smallest to largest

Family Members   _____

Strangers   _____

Kind of Knows/Social Circle   _____

The largest group of attackers is kind of knows, such as friends, classmates, coworkers, neighbors, coaches, and other nonfamily members who are trusted and have moderate access. Family and relatives are those who have easy and frequent access; they are the second largest group of attackers. Strangers, the most commonly feared group, are actually the smallest group of attackers, though assaults by strangers are typically more brutal than attacks by the other two groups. There are about 750,000 registered sex offenders in the U.S., and about 250,000 of them are under supervision of a correctional agency. That means about 500,000 offenders are on the streets.

Who Attacks

men you know	80%
strangers	20%

Are all attacks basically the same?

No. There are two types of assaults. Assaults by men you know represent about 80% of all assaults, follow a CIA pattern (Connect, Isolate, Attack), and are less violent. Assaults by men you don't know represent about 20% of all assaults, follow an AIA pattern (Abduct, Isolate, Attack), and are more violent.

When do attacks happen?

70% of assaults occur between dusk and dawn.

Most attacks happen around:

House / Apartment / Hotels
Parking lots / Parking ramps / On street parking
Dusk to dawn (70%)

Where do they occur?

Over 50% of all attacks happen in homes, apartments, dormitory rooms, and other places where victims feel safe and drop their guard. The next most common place for attacks is around cars in places such as parking ramps, parking lots, parking garages, and on-street parking. The most common places for assaults by strangers are mall and grocery store parking lots.

How does it happen?

The most common tools used by attackers are alcohol, drugs, and emotions, such as fear, shame, and guilt that lead to temporary confusion. Weapons, such as guns and knives, are used in a little under 10% of all assaults.

Can I ever leave my house and be safe, or do I have to be a hermit for the rest of my life?

You cannot control the actions of others, but you can take control of your life by managing what you do to be safer. We will explain how to prevent or avoid an assault and escape if the worst happens. You can take control, live the life you are meant to live, and be safer doing it.

Break out of the bubble of denial and listen to the information we offer you. That's the first step in taking control. Though the topics we discuss are intense, there is much good news.

Using Lessons from
the **EMERGENCY ROOM**

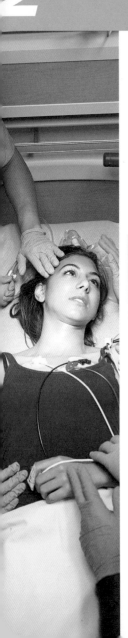

chapter 2

Using Lessons from the EMERGENCY ROOM

Emergency room doctors and SAFE nurses (Sexual Assault Forensic Examiners) describe two common denominators among assault victims they treat:

> 1. About 90% of the cases involve alcohol or drugs.

> 2. About 95% of victims say something like, "I had a bad feeling before it happened."

#1 Contributing Factor is Alcohol and Drugs

90%

TIPS:
- Know your tolerance
- Protect your drinks
- Buddy up

Had a Bad Feeling Before it Happened

95%

Let's understand these two common themes to be safer. First, we'll explain how alcohol and drugs play into attacks. Second, we'll explain how to recognize and react to warning signals prior to an attack.

90% OF CASES INVOLVE ALCOHOL OR DRUGS

Understanding Alcohol

Alcohol is a big part of social gatherings. It is commonly the center point for hanging out. We may have a glass of wine with dinner or a few beers while watching the game. Coworkers and friends often salute the end of the week with a happy hour. We use alcohol to help us relax, to decompress after a stressful week, or simply to give us something to do while we spend time with the people in our lives. When we use alcohol here is what happens:

1. *We become less aware.* We lose track of time, blow past our self-imposed curfews, don't notice when the person next to us leaves and someone else takes their place. We stop keeping track of our drinks or even where we put them. That's being less aware.

2. *We become less inhibited.* Wallflowers hit the dance floor, a co-worker suddenly becomes a comedian, or a friend initiates an arm-wrestling contest with strangers. Things that may have

seemed outrageous become comedic fodder. Maybe you've had the "oh crap" moment when you woke up the next morning and remembered telling your boss what you really thought. That's being less inhibited.

3. *We become more willing to initiate contact.* We become friendlier, more flirtatious, more willing to let go of our intimate inhibitions. "Liquid courage" allows someone to finally talk to a person they've had their eye on. A group of happily married women may be more willing to chat up some guys at a bar after a few drinks. Couples just starting to date may suddenly be rounding the bases faster than they ever had. That's being more willing to initiate contact.

4. *We become more aggressive.* Are you more likely to start an argument with your significant other before or after some drinks? Are you more likely to tell someone off while sober or tipsy? The problem with alcohol is that it eliminates our filter. We say what we mean, and we say it like we mean it. That's being more aggressive.

These reactions apply to both men and women, but aggression is particularly important in men's behavior. They are more willing to get loud, start shoving, and get physical, resulting in fights. They are also willing to get physical with women to get what they want. Let's say a guy and girl are going to intimate places they maybe wouldn't have gone to sober. If the girl suddenly decides to change her mind, the male can get aggressive when the action stops. This is the starting point for many date rapes.

Alcohol is the rape drug of choice. It is inexpensive and easy to obtain. Drinking is commonly accepted. If a potential attacker can get one drink into a woman, the second one is easier. Then the drinks can get stronger and go down faster. Soon she is unaware and uninhibited. The trap has been set, and she is in it.

Ask yourself why fraternities offer free alcohol. Ever wonder why college guys throw parties with $5 admission and let total strangers into their house to party? Why are guys so willing to buy drinks for women? The answer is simple. Offer free or cheap alcohol and people will flock to your door. They let the alcohol do the work. Alcohol makes her unaware. Alcohol gets her less inhibited. Alcohol makes her flirtatious and willing to go places she normally wouldn't go.

Imagine a female and male in a social setting. It could be a happy hour, could be a wedding, or could be a gathering for a friend. It's getting late, everyone has had a few drinks, and everyone is having a great time. Two people notice each other from across the room. They like what they see. There seems to be immediate sexual chemistry. Here is what is playing in their minds.

HER:

IDEA 1. He is smoking hot.

IDEA 2. I wonder where he goes to school, or what he does for a living.

IDEA 3. Give me something we have in common: Indy music, rock climbing, foreign movies, Mexican food cravings, ANYTHING!

IDEA 4. Please, please, please, don't be allergic to cats.

HIM:

IDEA 1. She's smoking hot.

IDEA 2. How do I get some of that?

They talk. Turns out he loves Indy music, did a semester abroad, and speaks fluent French. The girl is smitten. They flirt a little, and he asks her if she wants to go listen to an up-and-coming new band. They go upstairs, to his car, or head to his place to do so. She feels comfortable with him and lets him get closer. He gets closer and likes it. He's hoping for more. At some point he begins to cross physical boundaries she has set for herself.

Depending on his personality and his reaction to alcohol, there are three ways this can go:

1. She can say something like, "That's far enough for to-night," and he could stop.

2. She could say "that's far enough" and throw in some physical resistance, heated language, or both, at which point he could stop.

3. She says stop and resists, but he's not happy with that and starts to press for more contact. This pressure could come across as calm and collected. "What's the big deal? We're just having fun. Everything is fine. Just relax and have some fun." Or it could start to get scary if he begins applying physical pressure to make her continue.

She is at a critical decision point. She may feel confused because she was just interested in seeing if they had a good connection. She may feel ashamed for letting herself get into this situation. She may feel afraid that he will hurt her if she resists too strongly. But going to the next level of close contact is not what she had intended.

What happened? Alcohol helped get the story started. It made her more willing to initiate contact, less inhibited in her initial actions, less aware of the circumstances that were developing, less aware of boundaries that were being crossed, and less able to cope with his aggressiveness. Alcohol made him less inhibited so he initiated and pursued contact with her, wanted physical contact so he isolated her, and wanted more physical contact so he pushed her up to her boundary.

Variations on this sequence of events happen all time. The prevention and escape techniques in this book will allow you to cope if you ever find yourself in a situation similar to this.

Understanding Drugs

Sexual assault linked to drugging may be the most unreported crime in America. Drugs are significantly different than alcohol. Someone under the influence of alcohol will have fewer inhibitions and diminished awareness than normal. They fade in and out, remembering portions of what happened. But someone who has been drugged will be totally uninhibited, totally unaware, and totally compliant regardless of their normal boundaries, remembering nothing of what happened.

Karen was at a frat party. She was a Division 1 athlete who didn't party much due to her team's travel schedule. Although she would typically be fine after one or two drinks, she started to feel disoriented during her second drink. One of the fraternity members came up to her and said she looked as though she could use some fresh air. Karen agreed. Once outside in the courtyard, she found herself up against 10 guys in a semicircle with a guy in the middle who had his pants down. He demanded oral sex. Though her mind was fuzzy, she made a wisecrack, turned around, and ran back into the party headed for the restroom. He followed her into the room and locked the door. Karen's friend Tasha saw her looking panicked and followed her toward

the restroom. She pounded on the door, screaming at him to open it up and let Karen out. He stopped the assault, opened the door, and walked casually away as though nothing had happened. From that point on, Karen remembers nothing about the rest of the night. They went to Tasha's apartment, hung out for a while, but Tasha took Karen home because she was acting so weird. Karen had been drugged. It wasn't reported. If the guys had waited a few more minutes, she would have been compliant in the courtyard, doing whatever they had in mind. In the morning, she wouldn't remember any of it. The story could have had a tragic ending. The guys got away with drugging Karen, but her friend saved her. **"**

For predators, drugs are the best vehicle to get what they want. Drugged victims are awake, responsive, and willing to participate in extreme sexual activities regardless of their normal standards. Victims can't put the "who, what, when, where, and how" pieces together, so they often don't go to law enforcement because they can't answer any questions satisfactorily. The attackers get away with it, and the victims live with the consequences. Given the ease of creating video images and the pervasiveness of social media, victims can suffer immensely painful consequences from photos or videos where they were participants but had no awareness of what was happening.

" *Ann's neighborhood was fun. She and her husband hosted parties as did their friends. Ann attended a summer party alone because her husband was away. She was sipping lemonade. One of the neighborhood men saw Ann's drink was nearly empty and offered to freshen it up. She had a few sips and continued visiting with friends. Soon Ann began to feel a little tired and a little dizzy, so she decided to call it a night. The neighbor man offered to walk her home. She said*

> *she was fine and could get herself home. He insisted saying,
> "It's the gentlemanly thing to do." At that point one of Ann's
> female friends interceded and said that she would walk her
> home. The man pressed on saying that he would be glad
> to do it, but Ann's friend was resolute that she would take
> Ann home—and she did. Ann got to her house, went inside,
> locked the door, sat down, and she doesn't remember any-
> thing until the next morning. She had been drugged and
> had a close call. It was not reported.*

Rohypnol, ketamine, GHB, and even Visine eyedrops are all effective drugs. They are easy to obtain if a predator knows where to look,
and they are easy to administer. Lacing alcoholic beverages is simple
and commonly done, but something as benign as bottled water can
be loaded using a fine gauge needle and injecting chemicals through
the plastic cap. Tactics such as those are almost impossible to detect
or stop. Drugs can be injected into juicy fruits and applied to most
foods. Once applied, they essentially disappear. Depending on body
weight, the amount of drugs used, and how much is ingested, the
victim will begin to feel the effects in about 10 minutes. Soon after
that, they will become totally compliant, doing whatever the predator
suggests. The victim will remain awake, active, do whatever is asked,
and won't remember any of it.

 > *Sue and her husband were on the river with their boating
> friends. It was getting late, and her husband decided to head
> back to their boat for the night. Sue decided to stay with their
> friends and have more fun. She does not remember what hap-
> pened about halfway through the evening, but she woke up
> the next morning undressed and in a hotel room. In her purse
> were notes describing wild sexual things she had done. She
> didn't know if pictures or videos had been taken. She didn't
> know who was involved. She was frantic about what may have*

happened and afraid to tell her husband. It was not reported and someone got away with it.

Katie got a call from her mother and sister. The background noise was loud, they were being boisterous, and they asked Katie to join them at a local sports bar. They had just come from a baseball game and stopped there on the way home. Something didn't feel right. Katie's mom did not go to bars—ever. She sped to the bar. When she got there, her sister and mom were in a back room surrounded by men, and things were happening that Katie couldn't believe. She went nuts, yelled at the men, and dragged her sister and mother out of the place. They hit the couch at her apartment, upset that she had spoiled their fun. Six hours later they came to and didn't remember anything that happened after they got to the bar. They were horrified and mortified by what she described. It was not reported, and someone got away with it. **99**

This is reality for both teenagers and mature women. There is good news. It can be prevented. We will explain how to be safer in subsequent chapters.

"I HAD A BAD FEELING BEFORE IT HAPPENED"

Gavin DeBecker wrote an excellent book, *The Gift of Fear*, totally devoted to exploring this topic. Here is our brief version regarding this incredibly important point.

Navy SEALs trust their feelings about danger and depend on their instincts to stay safer. Almost daily a scenario such as this happens. Here is an excerpt from *Damn Few* by Denver Rorke: "We were on the way to a target. All of a sudden, 'Shift right!' the lead driver shouted over the radio. Everyone stayed with the lead guy, even though we didn't know where he was going or why. 'What the hell was that?' 'I don't know,' he said. 'It just didn't feel right.' Everyone understood exactly what he was talking about. Everyone was 100% good with that."

When I was an officer in the SEAL Teams, if one of us felt something just wasn't right, we all responded. Even if our team member couldn't explain why he felt that way, we trusted his feelings. When that feeling was present, we didn't question it; we changed our course of action. If hard-charging SEALs honor their feelings as a way to avoid danger, you may want to do the same thing. These feelings are not a sign of weakness. They are part of strength. They help us be safer.

We all have something inside us that warns us about danger. It's that feeling we get when something just isn't right. Our Not Me Team calls it our "Creep Meter," but it has many other names: survival instinct, feminine intuition, guardian angel, gut feeling. Some feel the warning in their gut; some get a chill up their arm or in the back of their neck. Others may get a dry mouth or a sudden headache. Regardless of how or where you get the feeling, when your Creep Meter goes off, something isn't right. The wise course of action is to get away.

If you spend time with animals, this gift is apparent. They have a sense that tells them when something isn't right. When they feel it, they don't wait to see what the threat is; they get away immediately. We have that same gift, if we listen.

Can you remember a time when something just didn't feel right about a person? You couldn't explain exactly what bothered you, but something just didn't feel good when you were near that person or interacted with them. After a period of time, you learned something about that person or had an experience with that person that was painful, difficult, or troubling. When I ask people about this feeling, they can always remember a situation such as this. Somehow their Creep Meter knew something was wrong—and it turned out to be correct. Your Creep Meter can be activated by a person, car, bar, restaurant, building, street, path, boat, or just about anything. If you feel it, there is a potential problem.

About 95% of emergency room sexual assault victims describe "having a bad feeling" before the attack happened.

We have a natural tendency to deny or overthink our Creep Meter. To avoid admitting we live in a dangerous world or to avoid realizing we may be in a threatening situation, we hush our Creep Meter to feel safe. Most of us prefer to not recognize danger until it becomes undeniably real. We spin information in a way that makes us feel better.

Imagine that you are walking alone at dusk. You approach a man standing idly by himself on the sidewalk, talking on his phone. There may be a twinge in the pit of your stomach, or you may feel a brief moment of tightness in your neck or shoulders as you process what you are seeing. You work to find a reason why he is there. A common reaction is to deny or not honor the Creep Meter and make the situation feel OK, creating explanations for why you are still safe:

- Maybe he's waiting for a friend and they decided to meet there.

- Maybe he's stopped to have a cigarette.

- Maybe his dog is taking a leak in the bushes.

- Maybe he has bad cell reception and finally found a hot spot.

- Maybe his wife and he had an argument and he's blowing off steam.

The ideas are becoming more irrational as the distance narrows, but you're grasping at straws to feel safe. Your mantra becomes "This is fine. You're being paranoid. This is fine. You're being paranoid."

My wife encountered a situation like this. Although she felt a little weird about what she was seeing, she continued to approach the man rather than turn around or cross the street. It turned out he was a predator. He tried to grab her. She got away, but he chased her. In the end, she escaped, but if she had honored her Creep Meter and avoided getting close to him, she could have avoided the dangerous situation. The lesson here is DO NOT deny the Creep Meter. DO NOT try to make the situation feel OK by rationalizing.

You will face a complicating factor called "social programming." Simply stated, social programming is a bunch of rules our culture and community have taught us about how to behave. Those rules focus on not hurting people's feelings, not embarrassing ourselves or others, not making others feel uncomfortable, giving people the benefit of the doubt, respecting our elders and people in positions of authority, and obeying many other behavior guidelines. Regardless of what culture we are in, there are a bunch of rules we are expected to play by in order to remain a member in good standing within our community.

You need to understand social programming, because it can make you less safe when your Creep Meters goes off. Following the rules can lead you to second-guess yourself when an older person or a person in a position of authority asks or tells you to do something that just doesn't feel right. A conflict can develop between the action you want to take to be safe and what your social programming has conditioned you to do. Your Creep Meter is warning you to get away, and your social programming is telling you not to be rude, disrespectful, or to hurt someone's feelings.

What should you do to be safe? The answer is simple—GET AWAY! You will want to follow your social programming, deny the reality of the danger, or overthink the situation. If you do that, you help the predator get closer and you get deeper into a situation you don't want to be in.

Go back to the man on the sidewalk and turn him into a woman. As you are out walking, you approach a woman standing idly alone on her phone and your Creep Meter goes off. She feels wrong for some reason. Are you likely to deny or rationalize the threat because it's a woman? We are programmed to not think of women as threats, but women sometimes hurt other women. If your Creep Meter says there is something wrong, the only safe action is to GET AWAY.

WHAT DOES GET AWAY LOOK LIKE?
SCENARIO 1

While you are in a social setting, someone trips your Creep Meter. They want to engage in conversation, but something about the person feels off. The appropriate GET AWAY action may be to simply excuse yourself to make a phone call, or use the restroom, or say your coworker just arrived and you've been waiting for them. Then move to another part of the room.

SCENARIO 2

After working late you head to your car in the parking ramp. While digging through your purse, jacket, or pockets to find your keys, you look up and see someone approaching who trips your Creep Meter. The elevator doors are closed, and the stairwell is far away. You can't get to your car before he gets to you. The appropriate action may be to yell, "Get away from me!" and run to an exit or the first place you expect to see people.

Match your reaction to the circumstances. When moderate action is all that is necessary, be moderate. When loud, strong action is appropriate, scream and run!

This is one of the most important points we want to make: IF YOUR CREEP METER IS GOING OFF, GET AWAY. The best way to stay safe is to create physical separation from whatever caused the feeling. You can spend as much time as you want afterward analyzing what happened and what tripped your trigger.

A member of our team is a SAFE nurse. She has supported assault patients in emergency rooms for many years. It is heartrending to her when she hears the details of assaults and somewhere within the description the victim mentions having a feeling that something bad was going to happen. Their Creep Meter went off, but they didn't have information to understand what to do about it.

Here's all you need to know:

You possess a powerful tool for staying safe. Use it. Honor your Creep Meter and GET AWAY when the signal goes off.

UNDERSTAND THE CRITICAL DECISION POINT

But what if you can't get away? Your Creep Meter is going off, you want to get away, but you can't see a way out. Perhaps you tried to get away but you got stuck or trapped. This is what we call a "Critical Decision Point." What should you do?

There are two basic choices:

1. *Prepare to fight.*

   Sounds like, "Not Me! No way. I will not be a statistic. I am going to resist with all my might because I know this is the best place to stop this." This choice may include yelling and swearing at the attacker, running away, or using the escape moves we will teach you.

2. *Prepare to cooperate.*

   Sounds like, "Please don't hurt me. I'll cooperate. I just want to go home to my family." This choice may include negotiating. Potential victims may offer up their money, car keys, phone, or valuable goods. They may promise not to tell anyone if the attacker lets them go. They cooperate in an attempt to come out of the worst alive.

In the chapter on assaults by strangers, we will give you data that describes the consequences of both these choices. Though both choices can lead to painful consequences, the data overwhelmingly show that choice 1 (resist) produces better outcomes. Our initial reaction may lead us to choice 2 (comply), because most of us want to avoid a fight. In the moment of the crisis, you may feel that cooperating (choice 2) and trying to negotiate with the attacker is better, because you want to live in a world where people help one another and you hope your offer of cooperation will moderate the attacker's behavior. Sorry. These guys don't work that way. They play by a different set of rules. A predator will see your attempt to cooperate as weakness and evidence that you will submit to his will. Your cooperation will allow him to get closer, take control, and do what he wants. The consequences of choosing to cooperate are typically tragic for the victim.

Choice 1 (resist) can lead to negative consequences ranging from embarrassment to physical injury. Screaming obscenities at someone approaching you could be embarrassing when the person ends up being a former classmate from high school who unfortunately went bald and gained a lot of weight. So you are a little embarrassed, but you are 100% safe. If you are forced to resist using the moves described later in the book, you may hurt your hand or wrist or be hurt by the attacker.

Neither option is risk-free. If you face an attack, you won't like either of your choices. One is bad, the other is worse. Remember, research and medical professionals tell us choice 1 (resist) produces a better outcome 85% of the time. Pick the bad choice, not the worse choice.

chapter 3

Defeating the Biggest
Group of ATTACKERS

chapter 3
Defeating the Biggest Group of Attackers

Why do these guys you know do this?

Data linked to the answer is vast and complicated. Our work has led us to the following thoughts.

DESIRE FOR SEXUAL RELEASE

Sex is different for men than for women. Moving past equality issues in matters of opportunities, careers, or compensation, men and women are different as relates to physical relationships and sex. To make this complicated subject easier to understand, reflect on the following:

   a. Several studies asked college-age men a question similar to this, "If you could have nonconsensual sex with a woman and know you would not be caught, would you do it?" 25–35% of men say they would. I found those results distressing and questioned them initially. After working in this topic area for quite a while, I believe the numbers are probably correct. But I had no explanation for this harsh reality.

b. I dug deeper to understand. Then I heard John Gray, researcher and author of multiple books, speak on male and female relationships. One of the conclusions I drew from reading his work is that in times of moderate stress and emotionally loaded activity, women have much higher blood flow to the parts of their brain linked to emotions than men do. That can partially explain why men and women can have such different reactions to intense emotional activities such as sex. Generally for women the emotional dimension of sex is broader, deeper, and more enduring than it is for men, because the event stimulates much more brain activity for women than for men. For whatever reason, men have less blood flow to the areas of their brain linked with emotion during these activities. Therefore men usually have a less intense, less complicated reaction to sex than women. Simply put, the event for men tends to be simple and linear—get from point A to point B driven by the physicality of sexual release. The event for women has many more dimensions involving emotional connections, sensitivity to the environment and social aspects of what's happening. One reality is not better or worse than the other—we're just different.

c. "John school" is sometimes a consequence for men who hire prostitutes. It is a court-ordered daylong session during which men are exposed to the tragic events that trap women in prostitution. Most men are shocked by what they learn and stop using prostitutes. What seemed like a simple money-for-sex proposition is now a form of slavery linked to complicated emotions. In our boys' and men's safety classes, we provide a segment where a woman who has been assaulted describes what happened to her and the deep, long-lasting negative impact the event had on her life. What seemed like a simple sexual event for the male was a life-altering emotional violation for the woman. In both John School and our classes, there are sometimes tears on the faces of men as they get a glimpse into the huge, lasting impact forced sex can have on a woman. That information changes them—and changes their actions.

d. We sometimes ask this question during class, "Ladies, can you have a significant intimate experience with a man that does not involve physical sex?" The ladies quickly nod their heads and respond yes. When we ask this question to men, their immediate response usually involves confused looks at us and one another. They don't quite understand the question. It's hard for them to separate intimacy from physical sex.

e. Another question we ask women is, "During an emotionally oriented interaction between you and your significant other, do you ever hear something along the lines of:

"Why are you making this such a big deal?"

"It's over. Let it go."

"Get over it."

The women respond with eye rolls and laughter as they agree that these are common responses. A big emotional deal for a woman is likely to be little deal for a man.

We offer these thoughts as part of a practical framework for understanding men's behaviors, not as an excuse for wrong behaviors. Connecting and intimacy for women is usually an emotionally loaded experience as she explores whether or not she has rapport with the guy. This same experience for guys is often driven by his simple, nonemotionally loaded desire for sexual release. In a social setting where alcohol is present and inhibitions are lowered, a man and woman can become isolated. If he pursues his interest in sexual release to the point where it is crossing the woman's boundaries, either her resistance is going to be sufficient to stop his momentum or it's not. This is a common date rape scenario. It is also a common scenario in assaults where men and women know one another but aren't dating. For him, it's often simply about stimulation and getting to the finish line. For her, it is often much more complicated.

DESIRE FOR POWER AND CONTROL

If a predator feels disempowered or feels his life is out of control, he may find temporary relief by feeling power over a victim. These predators may feel someone is out to get them—an employer, government officials, an ex-girlfriend or ex-wife, or any other person or group he perceives as persecuting him. He may feel that life has dealt him an unfair hand because of health issues, financial issues, or other challenges that feel overwhelming. In these mindsets, a predator may decide he will find relief if he has control over a victim, seeing that person submit to his will. If he can find a victim who will be immobilized by fear, shame, guilt, peer pressure, alcohol, drugs, threats, or other emotional leverage, he can set up an assault. In many instances the predator will use "grooming" techniques. These techniques begin with innocent-appearing touches on nonprivate parts of the victim's body. Over time, the touches migrate closer to private areas. When the touches finally become dangerous, the victim often feels ashamed or guilty for letting the situation get to that point. Complex feelings can result in confusion that leads to victimization. In some cases where family members, employers, or close associates are involved, these types of sexual assaults can continue over extended periods of time.

These predators may provide warning signs.

- Be wary of a person who talks like a victim, repeatedly speaking about "them" being out to get him.

- Be wary of a person who is critical or disparaging about other women in his life (mother, sister, ex-girlfriend, ex-wife).

Both of these behaviors can be preludes to danger.

WHO ATTACKS?

To simplify this complicated topic, we'll divide attackers into three groups:

1. Those you are close to: family members such as grandparents, uncles, stepfathers, stepbrothers, brothers-in-laws, or other relatives.

2. Those you kind of know: coaches and teachers plus acquaintances from work, school, church, the neighborhood, clubs, and sports.

3. Strangers

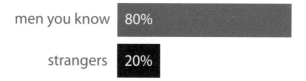

men you know   80%

strangers   20%

Groups 1 and 2 do about 80% of all assaults. If a bad thing is going to happen, it's probably going to happen with someone you know and don't perceive as a threat. That's hard to admit, but coming to terms with that information will make you more aware and safer. The good news is that nearly all of these assaults can be avoided or stopped by understanding the CIA sequence used in these assaults.

CIA

CIA stands for **C**onnect, **I**solate, **A**ttack. After analyzing hundreds of assaults and examining the personal stories women share in our classes, CIA is the recurring pattern that happens with attackers the victim knows.

From this moment forward the most likely attack you will face is a CIA sequence, and from this moment forward you will be able to identify steps in the sequence and stop it before the attack.

STEP 1: **CONNECT**

The attacker tries to establish an emotional connection that is closer than normal so your interaction with him becomes more personal. We see attackers using the following three techniques repeatedly:

Sympathy. Women are emotional, caring creatures. They are excellent teachers, nurses, counselors, advocates, service providers, and HR professionals. They fill these career niches because they tend to naturally care about people and their problems. That's part of what makes women special and wonderful. But it also makes them vulnerable. If an attacker can find a way to make a woman feel as though his problem is her problem, he gets more connected to her.

With younger women, the problem a predator offers can relate to parents, school, or popularity and may sound like:

- My parents just don't understand me.

- That teacher is treating me unfairly.

- I didn't get into the college I wanted. I feel like a failure, and I don't know what to do now.

- My girlfriend just dumped me.

- I feel like no one likes me or understands me.

With adult women, the problems can relate to work, health, finances, or relationships. It may sound like:

- It's tough. We've had some layoffs, so I have to cover two jobs.

- I'm working long hours, missing my kids' games, and not spending enough time at home, so my wife is mad at me. I have to work to pay for everything she wants. I can't win.

- I just can't seem to figure out how to make ends meet.

- My wife doesn't understand me. I try to make it work with her, but we just seem to be drifting apart.

- My brother is having health issues. We are very close, but he lives so far away. I wish I could be there for him more.

Women care. When they hear a boy or man say anything along those lines, they respond with compassion and start offering suggestions or encouragement to make the guy feel better. They do what seems natural. They talk it through to help solve the problem. When she does that, the attacker has accomplished step one. He's connected in a way that is closer than normal.

Flattery. Everyone likes to be complimented. Praising your looks, style, intelligence, athleticism, leadership—those all make a person feel good. It's easy to like the person offering the compliments. But if it goes on too long, you may start to get skeptical. "Yes, I'm amazing—but I'm not THAT amazing." When it starts to go overboard, you can sometimes sense this technique fairly quickly, even though you don't want to shut down the praise.

But flattery can be a little trickier. If he is complimenting you on accomplishments, the deception is harder to recognize. This may sound like:

- That's a really good test score. You are really bright. I could use a tutor like you.

- I had no idea you can do that. I'm in awe!

- That project was great. I bet you'll get the highest grade in class.

- Congratulations on your promotion. I was rooting for you.

You may want to hear more. If you do, his flattery is connecting you to him.

Listening. This is the most sophisticated technique and has trapped many smart, capable girls and women. Think about a topic that is really important to you. It could be your relationship with your parents, your child, a partner, a health issue, a death, your pet, a situation with a close friend, or a cause that is important to you. In the course of talking with a guy, the topic comes up and the guy listens to you. Really listens to you. He asks follow-up questions, and then he shuts up and listens. He asks about your feelings and then listens. Women say that men have many great qualities and skills, but listening and talking about feelings are not their strong points.

So when a guy asks questions with concern for a woman's feelings, that woman often can't help but feel connected. She feels like this person is a friend, someone she can trust.

Should you run for the hills every time a guy says something flattering or listens to you? Not at all. But it is important to understand that these techniques are commonly used to connect. If you want to know whether you are safe or not, ask yourself a simple question, "Am I safe?" You will get an immediate response inside. Trust it. If you get no reaction, you are probably safe. If, however, you get any reaction from your Creep Meter, there may be a problem. Go slow or get away to be safe.

STEP 2: **ISOLATE**

If he can CONNECT, it's time for step two, ISOLATE. He must get the victim away from people who can help her. Methods for doing this will seem nonthreatening. They may sound like:

- I really want to hear what you are saying, but it's noisy in here. Let's go outside (or upstairs, or out to the car, or for a walk) where it's quieter.

- It looks like we need more ice (or beer or chips) for the party. Let's hop in the car and get it.

- I have a new CD you'll love. Let's go listen to it.

- Let me walk you to your car.

- I'll walk you to your place (or hotel room) to make sure you get there.

- Want to go outside for a cigarette?

If he can find a way to get the victim away from people and help, he has accomplished ISOLATE and is set up for ATTACK.

STEP 3: **ATTACK**

Most of these guys have assaulted before. They've learned what techniques are most effective. People you know don't use weapons, but they commonly use alcohol or drugs. They also use emotional levers, such as fear, shame, guilt, confusion, embarrassment, or concern about others, that cause temporary immobilization. During this period of confusion—the bad stuff happens. If you are hearing anything similar to the comments below, cause a scene, an injury, or both to get away. If any of the comments below are going through your head, snap out of it. It's not your fault. Kick into gear and start protecting yourself.

FROM **HIM:**

- Don't make such a big deal of this.

- If you tell anyone in the family about this, it will ruin everything.

- Don't tell me you don't want this. You started this; now let's finish it.

- No one will believe you.

FROM **YOU:**

- How did I get myself into this? I should not have had so much to drink.

- My parents will kill me if they know I was here. I told them I was at the movies.

- This is my boss. If I resist, I could lose my job.

- If I cause a scene, what will everyone think?

The predator wants either sexual release or feelings of power and control, but he doesn't want either of you visibly hurt in a way that must be explained to the people you both know when you go back to the party, family event, neighborhood event, etc. After listening to hundreds of CIA stories, we absolutely believe the following is true:

You can stop a CIA attacker by getting mad and showing aggression. If this is about power and control, when you get mad and show a powerful response, he sees strength in you that he didn't know was there. "What are you thinking?" "This isn't happening!" "Back off you ___!" These kind of statements combined with red-hot anger at his outrageous behavior will nearly always stop these assaults.

If showing strength and rage doesn't stop him, the moves in chapter 5 will. The moves will produce surprise and overwhelming pain for him as well as visible physical injuries. We know of zero CIA assaults that continued after a victim used the moves on a CIA attacker.

Let's review the keys to stopping a CIA attack at each sequence step

CONNECT: Stop the sequence by trusting your Creep Meter. Alcohol dulls your Creep Meter, so proceed with extra caution in social settings where alcohol is involved. If you want to know whether you are in danger, just ask the "Am I safe?" question. Trust your immediate reaction. Do not overthink your response. No Creep Meter reaction is a green light to proceed. But both a little Creep Meter reaction (caution light) and a bigger reaction (red light) are signals to stop the sequence. Do not get isolated with that person.

ISOLATE: Perhaps you are uncertain about your reaction (caution light), but you want to get a little closer to the person to see if there is a connection. We recommend this concept: a little isolation for a little intimacy. If you want to talk to this person or get closer, but the room is too noisy, step just outside the room or move to the edge of the group. Give yourself a little separation from the crowd so you can have a little closer contact. If all goes well and your Creep Meter is quiet, proceed. If, however, he crosses any boundaries you don't want crossed, or if your Creep Meter reacts to anything about him, you are just one or two steps away from the group and help. Don't go upstairs, downstairs, out to the car, down the path, or anywhere else that is isolated unless your Creep Meter is quiet and you feel totally safe.

THE TEST. If at any point you are undecided about his intentions, give him the following test. The test is used to determine whether he is interested in just your body for the night or if he is interested in getting to know the whole you. The test offers him an option to see you again—during the day, when other people are around and alcohol is not involved.

- I think I like you, but I've had a little too much to drink and it's getting late. I have to be up early to (go to a meeting, meet a friend, get to class). I would like to see you again. Let's meet for a coffee break tomorrow (or meet for lunch or go to a movie next week).

The guy who is interested in the whole you will gladly take you up on the offer. The guy who pushes back with, "What's wrong? We're having fun. Relax. Let's keep going," and doesn't back off is just interested in getting some type of action tonight. This is an effective pass-or-fail test. You will know the results immediately. There are lots of fish in the sea. Move on if he fails.

ATTACK: If you become isolated and bad things are starting to happen, get mad, start yelling, and do everything in your power to get away. If he continues, use physical force and the moves to stop him.

SUMMARY OF CIA

The bad news is that CIA assaults (assaults by attackers you know) are approximately 80% of all assaults. These breaches of trust can be confusing and painful. Remember the differences between men and women. If something bad is starting to happen, it's not necessarily as intentionally hurtful as it may seem. Men act in a way that is natural for them. As a woman, you will be safer if you understand this and manage the situation accordingly. The good news is that understanding this information makes CIA assault attempts easy to stop. If the worst is happening, get mad, start yelling, and get away. Most guys are good guys and will stop. But if he persists, use the moves—they always work well on attackers you know.

chapter **4**

Defeating the Most
Violent ATTACKERS

chapter 4

Defeating the Most Violent Attackers

There are two types of attacks by strangers. In the first case, the attacker wants to rob the victim. If the attack is a robbery, get your valuables in your hands and then throw them one way as you run the other. If he goes after your valuables, the event is probably over. In the second case, the attacker wants to assault the victim. Here is information about these attacks.

Much of the information about CIA attackers pertains to AIA (**A**bduct, **I**solate, **A**ttack) attackers. The primary difference is that CIA predators don't want to physically hurt their victims because of the continuing relationship they will have with the victim and people they both know, whereas predatory strangers have no such constraint. In fact, AIA attackers may derive satisfaction from controlling victims by using violence to generate submissive behavior. This is scary. But, if the

worst is happening, you can use his need for power to defeat him. Really. We call the tactic for doing this, "Give a little to get a lot," and it's in chapter 5.

AIA (ABDUCT, ISOLATE, ATTACK) SEQUENCE
STEP 1: **ABDUCT**

Predators want their victims to submit. Submissiveness gives predators the power and control feelings they seek and makes forced sexual activity easier to achieve. During the abduct phase, predators "interview" potential victims to identify people who seem likely to comply and submit. The typical convicted sex offender has committed 50 to 100 sexual assaults before he is caught and convicted. These criminals have experience and know which characteristics lead to success. The most common characteristics predators say they look for are:

- Someone under the influence of alcohol or drugs.

- Weak eye contact—a woman who can't hold eye contact demonstrates a sign of submissiveness.

- Poor posture or weak sense of personal space—this can be interpreted as not feeling strong or empowered and not likely to defend oneself.

- Moving lethargically or with lack of intention—appearing lost, confused, or alone makes a woman appear vulnerable.

- Long hair—you go where your hair goes. If the attacker can get hold of your hair, the head and body will follow.

- Loose clothing—contrary to popular belief that attackers like tight, revealing clothing, they prefer loose clothing that is easy to get into or take off.

- Using a phone or wearing earbuds—situational awareness is impaired and the attacker can get close before being seen.

Regardless of which interview traits a victim does or does not demonstrate, never blame a victim. It is often inaccurate to assume the victim did something "wrong" that drew a predator's attention. The internal pressures that drive predators to commit their crimes build up during the interview period. At some point the predator may run out of patience and assault the next available person. In a case such as this, the assault attempt is unavoidable by the victim. Do not blame victims; blame attackers.

STEP 2: **ISOLATE**

We call the point of first physical contact the "x." That first interaction could be in a hotel hallway, behind an apartment building, or in a grocery store parking lot. Nothing good happens when the predator moves the victim off the "x." That first point of contact is usually the most public place the victim and predator will be. It is closer to potential help than wherever he plans to go next. Police often say that the body is found at the second location.

Variations of staying on the "x" include, "Do not get in the car" and "Do not let him take you to a remote place." All of this gets to the same point—don't allow yourself to be moved off the "x."

But if he is bigger, stronger, or takes you by surprise, how can you stay on the "x" and prevent him from moving you? Use our move called "Rag doll." It is simple and effective.

STEP 3: **ATTACK**

When the victim has been moved to an isolated location, attackers often begin by forcing victims to do things that are humiliating and submissive. Remember, these attacks typically are about the attacker's need for feelings of power and control. The victim may be forced to undress or perform oral sex. That is followed by a period of abuse that ends in ejaculation. When the attacker has achieved his sexual release, the attack is typically over.

But now he may face a dilemma. If he views the victim as a potential witness, he must decide what to do about that. The following graphic is an approximation of outcomes for AIA assault victims. Exact numbers are not known because reporting is imprecise, but we believe these numbers are approximately correct.

AIA Outcomes

The information in this graphic is disturbing, but it is intended to provide you with information that will help you decide which way to go at a Critical Decision Point. If you face an attempted assault by a stranger, you have two choices—resist or comply. One choice may lead to embarrassment or injury; the other leads to these consequences. One is bad; the other is much worse.

All the women in my life have seen this information. They have made their decision about whether they will fight with all their might or try to negotiate with an attacker. From the deepest part of my heart, I hope they have decided to make their stand at the "x," because both statistics and advice from medical professionals clearly say the best odds come from resisting and staying on the "x."

It's scary to make your stand verbally and physically. Women typically prefer not to fight. But if you choose to comply or negotiate, you are on the path to becoming one of those horrible statistics. Pleading for mercy gives him the emotional control he is looking for and makes you appear like the perfect victim.

The choice you make is totally personal. Every situation is unique, but the evidence about which choice tends to be safer is clear. Be brave and chose NOT ME!

Please pause right now to think about this information and visualize what you intend to do if faced by a predator.

chapter 5

You Can Escape If Something
BAD Is Happening

chapter 5
You Can Escape If Something Bad Is Happening

Remember, the first thing to do if something trips your Creep Meter is GET AWAY. Do everything possible to get away. If you can't get away, you'll need an action plan to escape that involves getting physical. All the actions you will learn in this chapter are gross. They are bad. But not doing them is worse. Here is how to escape.

THE MOVES

Many safety and self-defense classes are led by trained and well-intentioned people who come from a law enforcement or martial arts background. When we started the "Not Me!" training, I used my SEAL training as a frame of reference for teaching self-defense techniques. We taught the commonly accepted defensive moves: knee to the groin, heel of hand to the nose, finger-spear to the throat, kicks, etc. But a surprising thing happened. I approached women who had taken the training several months earlier and asked them to imagine their worst-case scenario where they could not GET AWAY. Then I rushed at them, giving them just one or two seconds to react. Only a few did a move that would have stopped me. Most didn't respond effectively because they had multiple choices and went through their options to select the best one for that specific situation.

> *Ro, one of our trainers, was a world-class martial artist, proficient in several disciplines. He had just won a tournament and was having a drink with friends at a bar. A competitor who was much bigger than Ro came up to him and made a very unflattering comment. Ro had a quick verbal retort. The big guy reared back and began a big swing. Ro was like a kid in the candy store. He saw the big man telegraph his punch. As Ro was deciding whether to drop him, dodge him, put him in the hospital, or just embarrass him, he hesitated before he started his move. Unfortunately, Ro's debate with himself lasted a little too long, and the big guy's fist was about to hit Ro's jaw. Ro started an evasive move, but the guy made a weak, glancing connection. Ro realized he knew too many options, and his delay selecting a move resulted in a lost opportunity.*

This story and my experience with past class participants forced a reevaluation of what we taught. Having too many choices leads to indecision. Indecision leads to delay. Delay leads to trouble.

The physical moves we teach must be simple so that any woman, regardless of her size, strength, or conditioning, can do them. They must:

- Be simple to learn so that women can acquire the skills in one session and be able to remember them later.

- Require minimal strength so that as life stages change, these skills can remain useful.

- Be reflexive so the move comes naturally when the victim is surprised.

After working with thousands of girls and women, we have created moves that really work. Now when I approach women who have taken the class, ask them to imagine being trapped, and then rush at them, they nearly always do our signature move, the "Cat Move," and can escape from me. Mission accomplished.

Navy SEALs, FBI Hostage Rescue Teams, and police SWAT teams all build their tactics around a winning principle: Use surprise and overwhelming force to defeat the enemy.

- **SURPRISE**: These teams attack when the enemy is not expecting it.

- **OVERWHELMING FORCE**: They employ noise (flashbang grenades, loud verbal commands) and big perceived presence to get the bad guys to give up rather than fight.

This same concept works for women who face attackers. The best way to win is to use surprise and overwhelming pain to create an opportunity to escape.

As we proceed, remember the lessons from the ER and DOJ statistics. Medical professionals and victims believe that "resisting leads to better outcomes than not resisting."

EYES

When we ask our class participants what they are going to do to escape from an attacker, we consistently hear from most of them that they plan to kick him in the groin. If you ask men what women are most likely to do, the answer is the same. Most attackers believe they must protect their groin. They can do that by staying up against the woman at the hip so she can't get her knee up or by keeping the woman at a distance so her knee can't reach his groin.

The most sensitive part of anyone's body (male or female) is their eyes. Have you ever scratched your eye or had something fly into it unexpectedly? Do you remember the pain and how you reacted? When an eye is scratched or struck, the person immediately brings both hands to the eye that has been hurt. We can't help it. We always do it. It's true for everyone. Anyone with an injured eye is going to be dealing with the pain. Everything else becomes secondary. If a potential victim can injure the eyes of their assailant, the assault is over. The attacker is out of the game.

While striking eyes is your best option, there is another highly effective and simple tactic if you can't get to the eyes.

BITING

In most martial arts, biting is a no-no. In the real world, biting is a powerful tool. Let's cover biting from the top down.

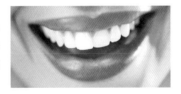

CHOICE 1: **TONGUE**

We've all bitten our tongue and know the excruciating pain that follows. Nothing exists in the whole world except the unbelievable pain in your mouth. Your hands came up to your mouth, and you try to figure out how badly you are hurt. For a little while your eyes are closed, and you focus on nothing but the pain.

When an attacker kisses you, he becomes immensely vulnerable. If you can lure him into kissing you, you can take control. We know this is gross, not an action you want to be doing, but at this point you will have done everything possible to GET AWAY, and if you don't stop this attack sequence, it can end very badly. So this is one of those bad choice/worse choice situations. Opt for a bad choice now rather than face a worse outcome later. Whether he kisses you or you kiss him, his tongue ends up extremely vulnerable, and you can take control using surprise and overwhelming pain. You win!

CHOICE 2: **THROAT**

Put your fingers on your Adam's apple. Quickly push in (be careful). Ouch? Throats are not only sensitive, they are vulnerable. Imagine if someone bit your Adam's apple as hard as they could. Your reaction would be to bring both hands up to your throat as you tried to breathe and figure out how badly you were hurt. It's likely your eyes would be closed if the bite was really hard. For a little while you would feel paralyzed until you were able to breathe again as the pain subsided. You can inflict that amount of pain on an attacker if he pulls you in close and you can get your mouth on his throat. Bite his Adam's apple with everything you've got. You can take control as he experiences surprise and overwhelming pain. You can escape. You win!

CHOICE 3: **FINGERS**

A person attended one of our classes and described an incident where the victim was grabbed from behind by an attacker. The victim screamed. The attacker covered her mouth. She opened her mouth wide, got one of his fingers in her mouth, and bit down hard. She bit his finger off and spit it out. He panicked, picked up his severed finger, and ran away. The victim used surprise and overwhelming pain to escape. Later she described the ability to do that as easy: "It was about like biting a crisp carrot."

If an attack is happening in a public place with the possibility of someone hearing you, you should be screaming as loud as possible. Your screaming will make him nervous, because it will bring attention to the scene. If he doesn't leave from the commotion, he may try to muzzle you by covering your mouth. That's your opportunity to take control. You can escape.

CHOICE 4: **GROIN**

Attackers demand oral sex both for sexual release and for feelings of power and control. As soon as his penis is near your mouth, bite down as hard as you can. To make the tactic even more effective, simultaneously crush his testicles with your hands. If a victim commits to the move and does it forcefully, she can create immobilizing pain. It is not a pleasant thought, but remember you tried to GET AWAY but couldn't. You are picking the bad choice of doing something you don't want to do in order to escape. The worst choice would be to go along and hope for the best by assuming he will show some compassion. Don't count on that. Create your escape opportunity by biting the unit and crushing the nuts. You win!

> " A mother of four took her youngest child out for a stroller walk. A van with four teenage boys inside pulled over to ask for directions. She answered, but they said they couldn't hear her. She was nervous but didn't want to be rude, so she stepped a little closer and answered again. A couple of the boys jumped out of the van and forced her inside. She was frozen with fear. They drove her to a secluded area and assaulted her for hours. One of the boys continued the assault by forcing her to perform oral sex. In desperation, she bit down hard. He screamed in pain, his buddies were shocked, and she was able to escape, running to a road where a motorist saw her. "

This woman felt overpowered and helpless. When her body and mind were so damaged that she felt she could endure no more pain, biting seemed like the only way left for her to resist. It worked. She thinks it may have saved her life.

 A teenage girl was trapped by a man who was forcing her to perform oral sex. He became increasingly aggressive, and she was terrified about what this would lead to. In desperation, she bit down hard, paralyzing him in pain. She escaped.

We have heard many variations of this story. While this tactic seems particularly gross, the results speak for themselves. It works. Regardless of a victim's size, strength, age, or physical condition, she can take control whenever she wants to if she bites down hard.

Put all four of these biting tools in your bag of tricks. The bad guys aren't expecting them. All you have to do is brush and floss regularly to keep your weapons ready.

SCREAMING

Escape is about surprise and overwhelming pain. Screaming can be a great tool if you do it right. Here's why:

1. **Surprise**. Attackers are expecting the victim to be immobilized by fear. With that fear often comes paralysis of voice. They are not expecting a woman to react with noise. If you can train your voice to react, you can cause surprise and gain the upper hand.

2. **Power**. Tennis players, martial artists, weight lifters, and anyone else who is mustering a burst of power will scream. It brings

energy from their core into whatever they are doing and generates more power.

3. **Call for help**. If there is anyone around, a loud scream can get their attention.

Some women visualize fear choking a scream in their throat. Our experience has shown that if a woman starts with a small scream as she practices her moves, she can easily progress to screaming more loudly. The most effective screams do not come from the throat; they start at your core near your diaphragm, flow up through your lungs, and burst out of your mouth. Play with this a little. Bring your screams up from your midsection. Start small and build up. You can do it. We play the way we practice and fight the way we train. So if you practice screaming from your core, it will be what you naturally do if you ever need to scream in the real world.

CAT MOVE

This is our signature move. Mother Nature taught it to us. Remember the Cat Move and default to it.

I was watching a little cat being threatened by a big dog. As the dog approached the cat, its Creep Meter went off and it tried to GET AWAY. But when it ran away, it became trapped in a corner. It crouched in fear, raised a clawed paw, and hissed as the dog closed in. When the dog's face got within striking range, the cat lunged,

screeched, and lashed at the dog's eyes and nose with both sets of claws. The surprise and pain from the attack caused the dog to turn and run away, tending to its wounds. The cat escaped.

Thank you, Mother Nature. You just taught us how a smaller, weaker victim can escape from a larger, stronger assailant. It isn't about the cat "winning" the fight. It is about the cat using surprise and overwhelming pain to escape from the attacker.

USING THE CAT MOVE

When we are surprised or scared by something, we instinctively lean away from the threat and bring our hands up to protect our face and head. It is a natural and reflexive reaction to danger. Let's call it the "I'm scared" position. We don't have to think about it. It just happens. When we get over shock and are in that position, we are perfectly set up for the Cat Move.

‹ CAT MOVE—"I'M SCARED"

CAT MOVE—EYE STRIKE

The Cat Move is simple. Straighten all ten fingers out, make them rigid, and spread your fingertips so there is a little space between them. You have just created ten rigid mini-skewers. From the "I'm scared" position, look at the attacker's eyes and make a hard thrust straight into them. Looking at an attacker's eyes may be difficult, but it will improve your accuracy. Just as focusing on a golf ball, tennis ball, dartboard, or baseball helps you hit accurately, the same applies here. If you look at his eyes, you'll hit his eyes. And if you do this move as fast as you can, the attacker cannot react quickly enough to protect himself.

Good reaction times are around one-half of a second. In less time than that, your fingers can travel the short distance to his eyes; he cannot react fast enough to block your move. His reaction time will be slower than your striking speed if you go first, fast, and commit to the move. The only question is when you are going to use it and take control of the situation.

The Cat Move is the most important escape tool in your bag of tricks. From first contact at the "x" all the way through an attack scenario, you can take control of the situation any time the attacker's face is within arm's length in front of you. The secrets to success are:

1. Commit to the move.

2. Go "first and fast," striking deeply into his eyes. It's gross and crude, but it can save your life.

Practice with a pillow to make this move reflexive. Have someone hold a pillow in front of you. Imagine it's an attacker's face. Go to your "I'm scared" position. When the pillow comes within arm's reach, jab quickly and with full commitment into imaginary eyes. With just a few repetitions, you can freshen up your best defensive move.

SIDE CAT MOVE

If the attacker approaches from your side, use the Side Cat Move. All of the information related to the Cat Move pertains in this move, except that the move is done with one hand and the strike is to your side rather than to your front. See the picture below:

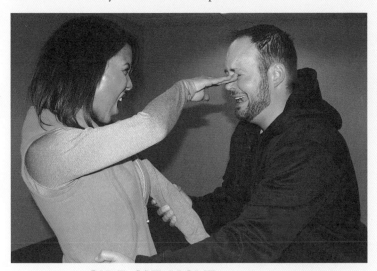

SIDE CAT MOVE—EYE STRIKE

Whether you are walking down a street or a hallway, getting in or out of your car, or walking past a place where an attacker is hiding, the Side Cat Move is easy to use. Assume that your arm is free on the side away from the attacker and he is grabbing you. Straighten your fingers on your free arm, look at his eyes, rotate your body, and jab your fingers into his eyes. If both of your arms are being held, just be a little patient, because soon he will release one arm to open a door, touch you, or do something that releases that arm. Then you can strike.

In all the Cat Moves, don't worry about whether he is wearing glass-es, because you are jabbing many fingers into two eyes and in the violence of the moment a finger will get to an eye. If necessary, hit him with a couple quick strikes. When you get one finger into one eye, the attack is over, and you can escape as he deals with the sur-prise and overwhelming pain.

OVERARM CAT MOVE

If an attacker gets close to you and wraps his arms around you or forces you up against a wall, use the Overarm Cat Move. Though your arms are trapped between the two of you, you need to free them in order to get to his eyes. This is easier than it may seem. From the starting position with your hands trapped between the attacker and your chest, slide both of your hands straight down the front of your body until your fingers are aimed at the floor. You may need to stick your butt out a little to make this easier. When your fingers are aimed at the floor, swing each hand out to

CAT MOVE–OVERARM

the side and raise each up so you can grab his ears. This isn't about hurting his ears; you are using his ears to get your hands in place so you can get to his eyes. When you grab his ears, stick your thumbs out into the middle of his face and they will be on or near his eyes. Now gouge his eyes with all your strength.

Common questions:

• *I'm short. He's tall. Then what?*

If you are shorter than the attacker, he must bend over to grab you. That brings his face toward you. When you swing your arms up, you reach above your head. Your hands can reach his eyes.

• *What if my thumbs won't reach his eyes?*

In most cases where your thumbs are a little too short, get your thumbs in place, then straighten your fingers and pivot them toward the middle of his face. They should be positioned to take out his eyes. Remember, it just takes one finger in one eye to cause the pain necessary for you to escape.

• *What if my arm or arms get stuck so I can't reach his eyes?*

Do the move with both arms. If one arm is stuck, use the other arm to attack. It's likely that one hand can get to his eyes. If both arms are pinned, be patient. Sooner or later he is going to release one of your arms to open a door, try to move you, touch you, or take clothing off. When that happens, strike his eyes with the free hand. If you have access to his throat while he is in close, use the Adam's apple biting technique mentioned earlier.

5

RAG DOLL

Attacks from behind are really scary. These attacks almost always involve the attacker grabbing the victim to move her off the "x" to a car, doorway, or other isolated area. As we explained in the AIA section (stranger assaults), the most important goal for the victim is to stay on the "x" and not get moved to the isolated location. The best way for her to not get moved is to quickly get her feet off the ground (so the attacker must carry her weight) by doing a move like a seat drop on a trampoline and extending her arms straight up into the air (so the attacker doesn't have anything to hold on to). When this happens, the victim slides to the ground and becomes almost impossible to move.

To understand the concept, think about the last time you tried to pick up a young child who did not want to be picked up. Most likely the child put its hands up and went boneless, like a noodle, on you. When that happened, you had nothing to hold on to, and the child felt much heavier than he really was. We call this move the "Rag doll." When a grown woman does it, she becomes an adult-sized version of that screaming toddler on the "x"—and that's the goal.

A variety of martial arts techniques are taught that involve grasping the attacker's arm and ducking under his armpit or other judo-type moves. Attackers can grab victims various ways, and these various attacks require different escape moves. For those who choose to learn these techniques, practice them, and

RAG DOLL

maintain the physical strength to use them, they can be effective. We choose to teach something simpler that any woman, whether she is nine years old, ninety years old, or nine-months' pregnant, can use.

Simple is better. Let's take a lesson from mixed martial arts fighters who spend much of their time learning how to win fights. When these fighters are getting tired or are losing a battle, they get onto their backs and bicycle-kick their feet so their opponent can't get at them. If you can replicate that technique, the attacker can't get at you, or he can't get at you without being kicked somewhere that hurts. If he gets hold of a foot, kick his hand with your other foot. If he tries to move around you, scoot around on your back, keep your feet aimed at him, and bicycle-kick. Very soon he will realize he can't move you off the "x." In any public area (parking ramp, bar, restaurant, public street, etc.), he will want to avoid being seen or heard. If you continue to cause a scene on the "x," he may get mad, swear at you, or kick at you, but he can't move you. He's looking for someone who will submit and not fight. You are doing the opposite. In case after case, these attackers give up and run away. Congratulations! You escaped!

RAG DOLL

Rag Doll: Dos and Don'ts

    Do: Surprise the guy by doing it quickly and with commitment.

    Do: Get your arms straight up quickly.

    Do: Get flat on your back with your legs up and kicking quickly.

    Do: Scream like crazy.

    Don't: Keep one or two feet on the ground because you are worried about hurting your butt. That type of bruise will likely heal; the effects of an assault may not.

    Don't: Put your arms out to the side so he has something to catch you with on the way down.

    Don't: Sit upright while on the ground so he can grab your hair or get access to your head.

Practice this move using an exercise mat or other padded device to protect your butt. Tell your partner to grab you from behind and move you to someplace off the "x." Even if they initially grab you in a bear hug, their grip will loosen as they try to move you. When that happens, surprise your practice partner with the Rag doll. If you commit to the move and do it quickly, you will succeed. After several successful practice moves, your body will reflexively do the move when you are grabbed from behind. It's kind of fun to practice. Use your scream as you drop to add surprise and increase the strength of your move.

ARM/WRIST GRABS

Another technique attackers use to move victims off the "x" is an arm or wrist grab. If the attacker is bigger or stronger than the victim, this can be scary. A tug of war will usually go to the man. We aren't interested in winning a tug of war. We want you to get out of the hold. It is easy to escape using a quick arm curl. To understand how this works, have a practice partner grab your hand or wrist. A normal reaction is to pull away, but that technique often fails.

Instead of doing a pull away, do a quick arm-curl (bring your thumb all the way to your shoulder).

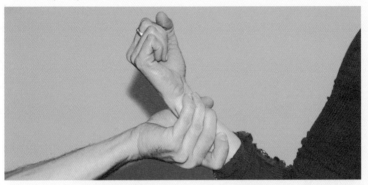

ARM CURL–FOR WRIST RELEASE

Here's why it works. In the first two-thirds of the curl, the attacker can maintain his grip. But in the last couple inches of the curl, as your thumb gets to your shoulder, the attacker's thumb is matched against your upper arm and shoulder muscles, and he can't continue to hold onto your hand/wrist. At this point, you lever out of the attacker's grip.

If the attacker is much stronger than you are, or if he grabs you with two hands, bring your other hand over the top of his grip, grab your own hand, and use both of your arms to do the arm curl. This two-hand technique has tremendous power and nearly always breaks his grip.

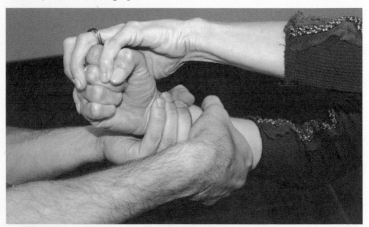

TWO-HANDED ARM CURL–FOR WRIST RELEASE

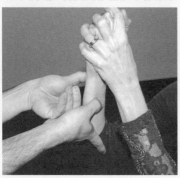

If the attacker grabs your wrist/arm/hand with both of his hands in some way that you can't lever out of with the arm curl, create surprise and overwhelming pain by using your free hand to do a one-handed Cat Move to his eyes. Do the move quickly and jab his eyes hard. He can't defend his eyes when both hands are on you. He will release his grip, both his hands will come up to his injured eye(s) and you can escape. Congratulations! You win again!

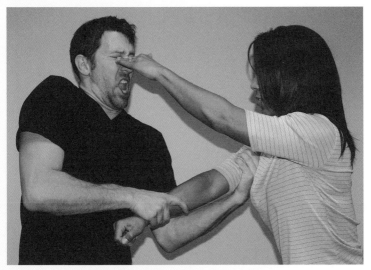

CAT MOVE—FOR WRIST RELEASE

GUNS AND KNIVES
If you want to know what sheer panic feels like, have a stranger point a gun at you or put a knife to your throat. Feel equipped for that? Probably not. Guns and knives are really scary. They are in that vortex of things you don't want to think about. Guns and knives produce the exact reaction an attacker wants them to if you aren't prepared to deal with them. Let's get you prepared.

As a SEAL I trained using multiple moves to disarm attackers. The problem is that there are too many variations in how an attacker can hold a weapon and approach a victim. Even when I was in great physical condition and training regularly, I was sometimes unable to react quickly enough when the attacker did something I was not expecting. I never became comfortable that I could handle the wide variety of possibilities I might face. Given that someone well trained in disarming techniques can get tripped up, it became crystal clear that we had to create a simple concept that does not involve extensive conditioning or practicing, because that is impractical given most women's personalities and schedules.

SITUATION 1

The attacker is approaching but does not have a grip on the victim yet.

When a victim suddenly sees a gun or knife as an attacker approaches, the response is typically to freeze in fear and go to the "I'm scared" position, leaning back with hands drawn up. We reflexively try to shield ourselves from the threat, so our hands come up. We are also typically unprepared for the shock of a gun or knife, so we freeze. This reaction is what he is expecting based on past experience. When "I'm scared" happens, he takes control and the AIA sequence begins. If the AIA sequence continues, roughly 90% of the time the victim will become part of the horrible statistics we outlined in chapter 3. If the victim can avoid "I'm scared" and immediately turn, scream, and run away, that will surprise the attacker, because turn, scream, and run is an atypical response.

IT'S THIS SIMPLE,
"GUN, RUN."

As the potential victim turns, screams, and runs, the attacker must react and decide what to do. He must think through his choices and pick one: discontinue the assault, pursue the victim, or shoot. The victim is not home free, but she is in a much better situation than a few seconds ago because, statistically, attackers neither shoot nor pursue victims who turn, scream, and run away quickly. It's possible that the attacker could shoot, but it is hard to find cases where they chose to do that. Here's our theory: He is looking for someone who will submit, and this woman is doing exactly the opposite with her immediate, loud, and strong resistance—she is not what the attacker is looking for. Regardless of why they don't shoot, history says that they stop the assault, and the intended victim escapes.

You can condition yourself to be safer with visualization exercises. Imagine that an approaching stranger suddenly produces a gun or knife. See yourself immediately turn, scream, and run toward people or lights. The faster you condition yourself to react and move, the more time and space you create between the attacker and you. Your reaction time can be the difference between life and death. Make it as real as possible in situations relevant to your life: public transportation, walking your dog, heading to your car after work, jogging, walking down a hotel corridor, or loading groceries into your trunk. You will play the way you practice and fight the way you train, so train yourself in as many different scenarios as possible.

See it. Practice it. Win!

SITUATION 2

The attacker has a grip on the victim.

Somehow the attacker grabbed you. Perhaps you panicked and froze or didn't see him coming. He has a hold on you, and he has a weapon. Now is NOT the time to go Kung Fu Fighter. Sudden movements with a gun muzzle or knife up against you can result in a sympathetic nerve response (tightening up or flinch) that can cause the trigger to be pulled or the knife to cut. Bad outcome. Our escape moves should be made when the weapon is off you. You may need to be patient and wait for the weapon to come off. This could happen when he tries to open a car door or a door. It may happen when he tries to touch you, pick something up, or any other time when he needs both hands.

There are ways to influence getting the weapon off you:

- Don't open car doors voluntarily. Pretend to be immobilized by fear so the attacker must use the key or open the door himself.

- Have a pretend meltdown if you aren't already there. If your hands are shaking so badly you can't get the key in, he may lose patience with you and do it himself.

- During your meltdown, your hands could fumble with the keys and drop them. He may bend down and grab them.

- Do anything you can think of to get him to use both his hands so that the weapon is off you and he does not have a controlling grip on you.

- Be patient and wait. It will happen eventually.

When he no longer has a controlling grip and the weapon is off you, make your move. The Cat Move (front or side) is the best bet. If you go first and fast, he will be surprised and be in immense pain before he can protect himself. The weapon will either drop or come off you as his hands reflexively go to his eyes. Just as we reflexively go to the "I'm scared" position, he will reflexively put his hands where the pain is. Ever seen an injured football player on the field? If he's had a knee injury, his hands instinctively go there to grab the pain. If you've ever slammed your finger in a car door, bent down to grab something and hit your head on the counter, or had someone accidently poke you in the eye, you may remember your first

reflexive reaction was to put your hands wherever you were hurt to protect yourself and evaluate the damage. This is what will happen if you commit to the move. His hands will naturally move to his injury and nothing else will matter as he deals with his pain. Do the Cat Move hard and fast. Then escape, screaming and running toward people and lights.

CAT MOVE

SITUATION 3

The victim is isolated and the attacker has a weapon.

He has you alone. You feel completely intimidated or overpowered. Something bad is about to happen. You haven't figured out how to get the weapon off you.

Perfect. His aggressiveness will set him up for "give a little to get a lot." He won't see it coming, and you will create your escape opportunity.

Up to this point, our focus has been on ways for you to resist effectively. There may come a time when you are overwhelmed by a weapon or physical strength. Getting away has not worked. You feel as though you are losing the struggle. Don't give up. There is a way for you to take control. One of the tricks he never imagined is "give a little to get a lot." The tactic here involves giving him a little of what he wants in order to get a lot—your escape. Here's how it works.

How do you react when you are in an intense argument or struggle with someone and they suddenly give up? This could be an argument with a client, your boss, your significant other, a neighbor, or friend. The disagreement has been very heated. It's getting nowhere when unexpectedly your challenger says, "Okay, fine. I give up. Have it your way." What happens? You relax. There's no reason to stay all tightened up, so your body relaxes a little.

During an assault, the attacker and the victim are both struggling intensely for power. The attacker is getting violent in order to show dominance, but the victim is battling back. Suddenly the victim says, "Okay, you win. Please don't hurt me. I'll cooperate. I promise I won't fight anymore." If the victim makes the submission believable, the attacker will relax, feel a sense of dominance, and loosen his grip. The attacker wants to believe he finally has overpowered the frightened victim, but he's not completely willing to let his guard down. He probably needs more convincing.

You know what he wants. The victim can persuade him that she is submitting by doing some form of highly submissive behavior. Examples would include starting to unbutton her blouse, starting to unzip her pants, or starting to unzip his pants. If any of these or other submissive behaviors is done convincingly, he will relax even further and drop his guard.

Then what? As he relaxes and starts to enjoy his victory, his hands and the weapon will likely drop down. When this happens, he becomes perfectly set up for the Cat Move. His eyes are exposed. He cannot protect himself from a Cat Move done first and fast. He'll be surprised and experience overwhelming pain. His hands will reflexively shoot to his eyes, and he will be incapacitated. The victim can escape.

We know this is a hard concept. It will be very difficult emotionally to go to victim mode, even if it is only to set the attacker up. Turning into a victim may seem counterintuitive to everything we've mentioned to this point. But "give a little to get a lot" is another strong and effective resistance tactic that recognizes there may be times when you feel overwhelmed by the attacker's weapon or power. This tactic identifies what he wants (control over your mind followed by control over your body) and lets him think he is winning, so he begins to relax and drop his guard. When that happens, switch right back into full attack mode with the Cat Move or any of the moves described earlier. "Giving a little" demonstrates apparent submission from his perspective. Offering something he wants, whether it's seeing body parts, seeing undergarments, or believing in the possibility of oral sex, will create the opening needed to "get a lot," your escape. A peek at something private is a small price to pay for your freedom and the chance to see your loved ones again. "Give a little to get a lot" is a tactic of last resort, but it's a good one.

> Our class participants tell us that they have effectively used the following: **Front and Side Cat Move** when the attacker drops his guard, kissing and biting his tongue, getting close and biting his Adam's apple, oral sex and biting/crushing, distracting him and then hitting him with a weapon.

HERON AND FROG

Here's a really important piece of information. Look at the heron and frog sketch on the following page. We have a heron trying to eat a frog and a frog trying not to be eaten. There will be a winner and a loser.

You may think the winner will be the one who has the most brute strength. Or you may go for the underdog with the choke hold. Who is going to win?

We don't know who is going to win, but we are certain about who will lose. The loser will be whoever gives up first. If you give up, you lose!

Imagine yourself in a situation that scares you. Your version of the heron and frog is the nightmare that wakes you up at night, or the scenario that makes you nervous. Visualize that for a moment. Feel the anxiety. Now visualize what the attacker looks like. See his characteristics as clearly as you can. As he approaches in your mind, where is your head going?

You will certainly be scared—that's normal. But if you can't imagine how to escape, you have talked yourself out of resisting and you have chosen to comply. *You have another choice.* Visualize that same scenario. Now choose not to give up, look into your bag of tricks, and select the trick you will use to take him out. You have several biting options and several Cat Moves. If things get really bad, you can use "give a little to get a lot" as a set up for any of the moves. You only need to do one move with commitment. He can't protect himself, and you can escape.

If you give up, you lose. When you recover from the shock and horror of your situation, pick a trick. Commit to it and do it fast with a scream to add a little boost. You win again!

DON'T EVER GIVE UP!

IF YOU GIVE UP, YOU LOSE.

chapter 6

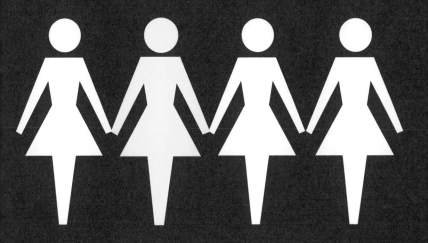

Safety
DEVICES

chapter 6
Safety DEVICES

A big myth we hear all the time is that women shouldn't carry a weapon because it will be used against them. Sure. That's possible. But statistically, it is wrong. Women have accepted it for too long, and it diminishes their ability to protect themselves. It's time for a change. Don't buy into the myth.

Over 10,000 women have attended our live classes. Not a single one—none—of those participants had an experience where either they or someone they knew was carrying a serious weapon and it was used against them. We have heard stories about victims without weapons who were attacked. And we have heard stories about potential victims who thwarted attackers either by threatening to use a serious weapon or actually using it. But we have heard no stories about potential victims who had a serious weapon and the attacker used it to complete an attack. I am discounting the few stories we have heard about how irritants such as sprays have been used to intimidate women. Though these devices are better than nothing, they are not as intimidating or effective as the more serious weapons. Statistically, it appears that occasionally an attacker is insufficiently deterred by irritants, but statistically attackers are effectively deterred by serious weapons.

If an attacker wants to use a weapon, he'll bring it with him. They aren't out searching for a woman with a serious weapon so they can use it against her. The typical convicted offender has 50 to 100 prior assaults. He has practiced. He knows what he intends to do. If that involves using a weapon, he'll bring it with him.

Remember the interview process. Attackers interview to find someone they think can be controlled and will submit. They are looking for victims. A woman with attitude and a serious weapon does not fit the profile he is looking for.

Fewer than 10% of attackers use a deadly weapon. If a potential victim has a serious weapon, shows it, and seems believable in her intent to defend herself with it, she has a psychological and physical advantage over the vast majority of attackers who are unarmed.

Deciding whether or not to use weapons falls into the bad choice/ worse choice arena. The thought of using a weapon against an attacker is probably terrifying to you. So is the thought of a weapon being used against you. But if you face an attacker, doesn't it make sense to stack the odds in your favor so you can stop him? For the reasons cited above, all the women in my life have selected one or more tools they choose to have around for self-defense. I hope they never have to use them, but I'm glad they have the tools.

Information leads to beliefs; beliefs lead to actions. If you believe that a woman has the right to protect herself, there are many safety devices she can use to do so. Put these tools in your bag of tricks so you can escape if you face danger.

ALARMS AND SCREAMERS

(+) No training needed

(–) Weak deterrent

(–) No stopping power

Be aware of the alarm in your car. Remember that a high percentage of assaults occur around cars. If your key fob has an alarm button, you have a very useful tool in your bag of tricks. Use it to clear the area if there is someone approaching or hanging around who trips

your Creep Meter. If the person is a threat, you will likely spook them. If they are not a threat, you'll have an amusing story for later.

ALARM

Also consider screamer alarms and attach one to your purse or key ring.

> *It was getting dark, and Stephanie stopped at a convenience store on the way home. Her car was isolated, and as she approached it, she saw a guy close by. He made a crude comment that was way out of bounds, and she got mad. She pulled the pin on the screamer attached to her purse strap as she simultaneously yelled, "You _____, get away from my car!" Startled by the shriek from the screamer and her aggressive language, he backed away. She was able to get into her car, lock the door, and drive away.*

PENS AND KEYS

(+/–) Modest stopping power

(–) Weak deterrent

(–) Requires willingness and ability to strike the attacker

If you are in a situation that makes you nervous, you can use a pen or a key as a weapon. Put the blunt end of the pen or key in the palm of your hand. Close your fingers on the shaft of the pen with two fingers on each side. You have created a very effective jabbing weapon. Replicate the Cat Move with the pen or keys in your hand. If you are trapped, attack first and fast by jabbing the pen into an attacker's face. As he deals with the pain, you can escape.

PEN

SPRAYS

(+) Very little training needed

(+/–) Moderate deterrent

(+/–) Moderate stopping power

Some friends at a party decided to test whether or not sprays are effective. One of them sprayed the device into a kitchen sink. The effects were so serious that the partygoers all had to go outside. Sort of spoiled the party. They learned that if you get a good quality spray anywhere near eyes or nose, the pain is amazing and nothing else seems to matter. That's the way it works with an attacker. Threaten him as a deterrent. Spray his face if you must. If the spray gets near his eyes or nose, it will stop him. No permanent damage, but amazing short-term pain.

SPRAY

HIGH INTENSITY FLASHLIGHTS

- (+) No training needed to flash it as a deterrent
- (+) Potential to gather DNA evidence
- (+/–) Moderate deterrent
- (–) Weak stopping power
- (–) Strength and practice are required to use it for stopping power

70% of assaults happen between dusk and dawn. Attackers like dark for obvious reasons—they don't want to be seen. High intensity flashlights can be used effectively in two ways. First, they create temporary paralysis when shined into an attacker's eyes, creating an opportunity for escape. Second, many high intensity flashlights have serrated edges near the lens that can create painful wounds if the victim strikes the attacker's face. If that happens, the flashlight can hold either blood or tissue for use in DNA sampling. Using the stunning intensity of the light takes no physical training, but striking an attacker requires strength and aggressiveness.

BATONS

(+) **Good deterrent**

(+) **Good stopping power**

(–) **Strength and some practice required to use it for stopping power**

When batons are closed, they don't appear threatening, but when the telescoping rods are extended, the tool becomes an awesome smashing device. Carry the baton in a purse, pocket, or have it ready in your hand if a scenario makes you nervous. If your Creep Meter goes off or a threat approaches, extend it using a quick wrist flick. Break things (hit a car window or strike a wall) as warning. And swing it back and forth quickly at shoulder level to defend yourself. It takes modest strength and requires aggressiveness, but if you are willing to be aggressive, the baton is very effective.

BATON

> Megan and her girlfriend had really enjoyed catching up at the party. At closing time, they decided to walk together to their cars. After a block, they had to go separate ways. As Megan approached her car, a man came walking toward her at a fast pace. Megan's hand was in her purse, holding her baton as she always did when walking alone to her car. As he moved toward her, she pulled it out, flicked her wrist, and snapped it open. He kept coming toward her. She yelled at him, "Get away from me!" He kept moving toward her and was getting too close. She swung the baton hard and smashed the plastic front on a newspaper stand. He jumped back at the noise and seemed surprised by her aggressiveness. Yelling something at her, he ran away. Megan called the newspaper folks the next day and explained what happened to their newspaper stand. They congratulated her.

STUN GUNS/TASERS

- (+) **Excellent deterrent**
- (+) **Excellent stopping power**
- (+) **Very little training required for both deterrence and stopping an attacker**

There are many types of stun guns. We will discuss those that are small, hand-held, have internal flashlights, and are rechargeable. Our female instructors really like these, because they are easy to carry and very effective. For use as a deterrent, aim the flashlight at the attacker's face. If the light doesn't deter him, zap the warning spark (it's a loud, bright spark between two electrodes) that is very intimidating. If that doesn't stop him, press the electrodes up against his skin or normal clothing and zap him. He will stop. A short zap (1 to 2 seconds) will temporarily paralyze him. A long zap (4 to 6 seconds) will cause his legs to buckle, and he'll go down. These are nonlethal (but hurt like crazy) and very effective. If you zap someone, you will have an opportunity to escape while he is recovering.

STUN GUN

> Deb and her daughter had gone to a movie downtown. It was dark, and they were walking to their car in a parking lot. No one was around except a man walking toward them on the other side of the street. He was a big guy and was wearing a hooded sweatshirt. He crossed the street, getting directly in their path. Deb's Creep Meter gave her a sudden stomach twinge. She put her hand in her purse and found her stun gun. She pulled it out, flicked the flashlight button on, and shined it toward his face saying, "Excuse me, sir. Please stay away from us." He said nothing and kept coming. She yelled, "Get away from us!" and flicked the button on the stun gun to the shock position. He said nothing and accelerated his pace toward them. When he was several paces away and still coming, Deb pushed the shock button and the night air was broken by a loud cracking sound and a bright flash between the stun gun's electrodes. The man jumped backward, swore at Deb, and ran away. Deb and her daughter ran to their car, locked the doors, and sped out of the parking lot.

GUNS

- **(+) Best deterrent**
- **(+) Best stopping power**
- **(-) Significant training required to store the weapon safely, carry it, and use it proficiently.**

A gun is the most effective deterrent tool. When serious people face serious danger, this is the tool they want to have. Attackers stop their assault attempts approximately 9 out of 10 times when victims show a gun and are believable about their willingness to use it. When attackers see the gun, they quickly learn their potential victim is ready to fight. She fails the interview, and the attacker retreats quickly. Though showing the gun is an effective deterrent tactic, the person showing the gun must be prepared and willing to use it if necessary. Using a gun moves into the lethal force area and is outside what we cover in this book. If you want to consider this option, be certain you get professional training from a reputable source, so you learn how to safely and effectively handle, shoot, and store the gun.

GUN

Dangerous Situations
and BEST PRECAUTIONS

chapter 7
Dangerous Situations **and Best Precautions**

Acomprehensive list of valuable precautions and safety tips would be very long. We will summarize the most important actions.

PARTYING
Have fun. Doing fun stuff helps make all the not-fun stuff worth doing. But so many assaults happen at parties that we want to share a couple more stories and some advice.

One of our trainers was at a party with her girlfriend. Both were very aware of party realities. To be safe while they had fun, they agreed to stay close to each other. They were at the bar standing back to back with drinks in their hands. Our woman set her drink down on the bar as she hugged a friend who had just arrived. Then she picked her drink up and continued talking to a guy she knew from church. A few minutes later she started to feel a little fuzzy. He asked her if she wanted to go outside and get some fresh air. She said, "Yes." She didn't remember her agreement to remain with her girlfriend as she walked out with the guy. She remembers nothing about what happened from the time she left the party until the next morning. Something happened—but she cannot remember what. After years, she still worries about what happened.

It only takes a moment to be moved away from safety. Going to the ladies room, the dance floor, out for a cigarette, or anything else that separates you from your buddy puts both of you at risk. Live your life and have fun, but do not leave your buddy alone, and do not let your buddy leave you alone.

A common practice is for a group to go out together and be a buddy group. This does not work well. When everyone is responsible, no one is.

A group of girlfriends went out together, agreeing they would keep an eye on one another. Halfway through the evening, Jen felt tired and decided to leave. She told a couple of the group members that she was leaving. On the way out, Patty said she wanted to go with her, and the two women left together. Several hours later, Jen's phone rang and one of the friends said they were very worried because they couldn't find Patty. Jen realized that the group of buddies had failed to keep track of Patty for a long time. Patty was safe, but she could have been in trouble and no one would have realized she was missing.

The buddy system works best when you have one buddy and both of you commit to stay in continuous close contact with each other. Have fun, but stay close together until you are safe.

CELL PHONES AND EARBUDS

We commonly hear stories from women who believe that being on their cell phone helps them avoid an attack. They assume the phone is protecting them, because they can scream and the person on the other end will know what's happening. This is exactly WRONG. Communication devices create danger rather than reduce it. Unfortunately, there are many surveillance videos that illustrate this fact. These videos typically show a woman on her phone as an attacker approaches from behind, grabs her, and drags her off. The person the woman was communicating with may realize something has happened, but the victim is gone and there is nothing they can do to help her.

Assaults happen quickly. There is no time for a description: "6' tall, medium build, brown leather jacket, bald, wearing black jeans, tattoo on his right arm, dragging me to the east end of the grocery store parking lot." It doesn't happen.

When we talk on phones, our situational awareness is shut off. We are immersed in our conversation and not listening for warning signals. As we text on our devices, our eyes are missing movements that could alert us to danger.

 One of our instructors believed talking on her phone was a good safety practice until she took our class. She would call her husband each night after work as she got off the train and walked to her car in the parking lot. After taking our class, she thought this through and realized her error. After making the change, she commented, "I can absolutely feel the difference. When I walk with purpose, head up, noting my surroundings and making it known that I am aware of who and what is around me, I see why I am now safer."

Being in the moment, rather than distracted on your phone, during transitions in and out of high-risk zones tells potential attackers that you are paying attention and makes you less attractive as a victim.

Earbuds work the same way. Our ears are one of our best assets for prevention. If you are listening to music while out running, you will miss the footsteps that are getting progressively closer and louder. You won't hear the stick breaking in the bushes and pay attention to what caused that noise that is out of place.

Try this: Walk up behind a friend who's on her phone and see how close you can get before she knows you're there. It's almost a guarantee you can put your hands on her before is aware of your presence.

That's dangerous when you are in a high-risk scenario.

Use your phone when you are in a safe building or are safely locked in your car. Stay off your phone in transition zones going to or from your car and whenever you are in a risky scenario.

CARS

Cars are a high-risk zone because they allow a quick transition from ABDUCT to ISOLATE. Attackers know victims will go to or from their cars sooner or later. Attackers can hide in cars. And they can force victims into cars quickly to begin the isolation phase.

The number one location for stranger assaults is grocery store and mall parking lots where use of cars is a common element in tragic stories. These high-traffic areas are filled with women running errands. Their arms are loaded with bags as they walk close to rows of cars. Their backs are exposed as they load children and bags into various doors on their cars. People walk closely behind them as they busily take care of their tasks. Amidst all these distractions and activity an attacker can easily approach undetected.

Though cars are a high-risk zone, they also lend themselves to many easy precautions and countless escape opportunities. Some of the easiest defenses and precautions are listed below. Do as many of these as you can while you go about your day.

Where to park

- Under lights
- By people: men and women together, families or women
- Close to the entrance
- In the get-away position for a faster, easier exit
- By the cart return so one side of your car is protected

Where not to park

- Far from the entrance
- In an isolated area
- By large objects
- By bushes/trash bins
- By a man sitting solo in his car
- By groups of guys
- By dark or shadowy areas

Additional precautions involving cars

- Gather your belongings while inside your car. Avoid being exposed in the transition zone.
- Turn off your radio and count to 10 so you can get acclimated to your surroundings before getting out.
- Get off your phone.
- Prepare your weapon of choice: pen, keys, baton, taser, mace, or pistol.
- Keep your doors locked at all times
- Get young kids in the car before you. You are better equipped to handle a threat than they are. Get them strapped in quickly, and avoid leaving them in the cart child seat so someone can use them against you.
- Buckle and unbuckle kids in the front seat after you are all inside and the doors are locked.

If you face an assault, react quickly so you don't get moved away from the "x." Do everything you can to not get inside the car. Use the Cat Move or any of the previously mentioned techniques. Remember, nothing good happens off the "x."

Perhaps there is a weapon involved and you can't make a move immediately. That's okay, you will have many options. As you move toward the car, say anything that sets you up to drive the car. Maybe he will buy a story about your car being hard to drive. Maybe there's alcohol on his breath, and you can tell him you will cooperate and take him anywhere he wants to go, but you should drive so he doesn't get pulled over for drinking. Fabricate any story that gets you into the driver's seat. Once there, you can crash the car near people and end the assault.

If you can't drive, there will be a continuous series of opportunities to stop the ISOLATE phase.

Imagine you are in the front seat, and he is walking around to the other side of the car. You can:

- Run from the car when he is at the farthest point from you.

- Honk the horn continuously to draw attention.

- Scream and make noise so passersby may hear you.

- Lock the doors.

- Call 911 if you still have your phone.

- Find a weapon: pen, high heel, anything you've stashed under your seat for protection.

- Most importantly, keep your head in the game. If you allow yourself to stay in panic mode for too long, you will miss many opportunities to get safe.

While seated together in the front seat, you can:

- Do the Side Cat Move to take out his eyes and cause an accident.

- Pull the steering wheel to cause an accident. Choose something to crash into while going at slower speeds: a parked truck, light pole, road sign, etc. The best way to do this is to use both hands and grab the top of the steering wheel fast and hard while sheltering your grip with your torso. If you only grab the wheel with your hands, he may be able to knock them off. It's much harder to push your hands off the wheel if you are using your whole body to cover your hands.

- Bail out of the car when it is moving at slow speeds.

If you are in the backseat, you can:

- Bail out.

- Reach around and take out his eyes while he is driving. He won't be able to reach you. Keep digging in his eyes until there is an accident and then run from the car.

If you are in the trunk, you can:

- Scream, kick, and make noise. If you can hear people, they can hear you.

- Search for the emergency release lever. Newer sedans are equipped with this feature. It's often illuminated for children to find it more easily. Know where it is in your car.

- Call 911 if you have a phone.

- Look for a weapon so you are poised to attack when the trunk opens. Even better, put a hidden weapon in your trunk. Some items to consider include a screwdriver, tire iron, golf club, high heel.

- Kick out the taillights and wave.

- Pull wires. Remember 70% of assaults happen after dusk. If you can cause the lights to flicker on and off or go out completely, a driver behind you may be concerned and call authorities.

• If the backseat folds forward, push it down and get to the backseat to either bail out or take out his eyes from behind, then escape.

• Most importantly—stay in the game. This is frightening to think about. If you spend your time in the trunk considering all the horrible possibilities that may happen next, you are wasting time and energy while he is in control. Use that time to gather your courage and formulate a plan of attack.

There are some cases where men intentionally cause minor traffic incidents to get women to pull over. If this is happening at night in an isolated area, do NOT get out of the car. The safest action is to not stop at all. Just wave your hand out the window, slow your speed, and get to a public place before dealing with the accident. There are also stories of attackers posing in police cars. If you are being pulled over in a remote area where you don't feel you've made a traffic violation, call it in to 911 and use the process above until you get clarification that there is indeed a police car in that area.

MUGGINGS

Muggings are either about your stuff or about sex. You will know very quickly which type of assault is happening.

> 66 *Mandy was close to the front door of her apartment. A man came out of the darkness and grabbed her. She yelled, "Okay, take my purse!" He yelled back, "I don't want your F'ing purse." When she heard that, she snapped out of shock and denial and realized what this was actually about. She started to scream and fight hard while he tried to drag her into the shadows. Her landlord heard the screaming. He yelled out his window and then came to her aid. The assailant ran off. She escaped because she chose to fight and make noise.* 99

Tips for muggings

- Throw your stuff one way and run the other. Create space between your stuff and you. This will cause the mugger to pause as he decides what to do, giving you some time to begin screaming and running away.

- Keep several small bills in your pocket to throw in one direction as you run the other way. You will begin to get separation from the attacker as he pauses to look at the money.

PLAN FOR SAFETY WHEN GOING OUT

- Whose your buddy? Your best protection against drugging is the buddy system. You and one or two friends buddy up. Remember that when everyone is responsible, no one is responsible, so don't rely on a group; pick a specific buddy.

- How to get home? Plan your ride home BEFORE you go out. Make a plan and stick with it so others know where you are and when to expect you.

- If you are walking at night, walk in groups.

- Stay on lighted paths and avoid shortcuts that involve isolated areas.

- Keep a weapon on hand, at the ready. It doesn't help you to have your mace buried at the bottom of your purse or backpack.

- Parents with college-aged daughters and sons, consider opening up an account with a local taxi cab company where your child attends school. Allow your child to use this account to get safe rides home at night. It's even better if one or two friends hitch a ride home with them. There is safety in numbers. The money you spend on them getting home safely is good insurance. It will get them in the pattern of planning a ride home and not letting people they "kind of know" walk or drive them home. It will also prevent drinking and driving.

- If someone is offering to walk you home, to your dorm or apartment, to your car after work or a happy hour, or to your hotel room when traveling, get on high alert. It's possible this is a gentleman trying to be polite and helpful. I hope that's the case. But if he's looking for an opportunity to attack, you can control the situation by allowing him to walk with you if it involves public well-lighted areas with people around. Stay out of dark, isolated areas. When you are still a moderate distance away from your car door, apartment door, dorm room or hotel door, give him a thank you and tell him, "I've got it from here. If you can just make sure I get in, that would be great." Give yourself several yards or more of open space where he can't get to you before you get in a door and lock it. Remember: The good guys get it, and the guys who may be a problem are the ones who resist this.

THE BUDDY SYSTEM

This is so important that we want to mention it again. Bad things may happen that you simply can't prepare for or avoid. Drugging is a huge problem. It goes far beyond college campuses. We continue to be surprised by the number and variety of drugging stories women share with us, such as from wives and husbands out at dinner, women at a black-tie events, women at neighborhood events, and the stories go on and on.

Drugging victims don't see it coming. We know that anything you put in your mouth can be used against you. The only effective defense we know of is to buddy up with someone who understands the reality of drugging and agrees with you that: 1) the two of you will get each other to safety immediately if the other starts feeling weird in any way, and 2) you will not leave each other until you are safely on your way home.

chapter 8

At
HOME

chapter 8
At **Home**

Though home is nearly always a very safe place, prepare yourself for those times when intruders can turn it into an unsafe place.

Intruders are very dangerous. A thief will enter your home when you are not there because he wants your stuff, not you. But intruders who enter your house while you're there may want contact with you. In the isolation of your home, very bad things can happen.

There are several simple actions that will make your home safer. You have probably heard the terms "hard" and "soft" targets. Hard targets are those that are prepared to deal with a threat. Soft targets are those that are not well prepared. Select any or all of the following actions to increase intruders' perception that your home is a hard target.

> **REMEMBER:**
> Over half of all assaults happen in or around your home or the homes of relatives/ friends/ neighbors.

PUT A SECURITY COMPANY SIGN BY YOUR DRIVEWAY AND SECURITY COMPANY DECALS ON THE MAIN DOORS

Whether you have a security system or not, the sign and decals will encourage potential intruders to look for a victim somewhere else that does not have a security system.

PUT A "BEWARE OF DOG" SIGN IN A VISIBLE PLACE

Whether you have a dog or not, intruders would rather not worry about the problem and will likely move on to a place without dogs.

PUT A MOTION-ACTIVATED SECURITY LIGHT ABOVE YOUR FRONT AND BACK DOORS

These lights are not expensive and are fairly easy to install. They turn your lights on when there is motion in the area around your doors. If an intruder is selecting a target, he would prefer one where he is not going to be performing center stage under a bright light.

LEAVE WINDOWS CLOSED ON MAIN LEVEL AT NIGHT

IN ADDITION TO MOTION LIGHTS, CONSIDER ALWAYS LEAVING YOUR FRONT PORCH LIGHT ON

IF YOUR HOME HAS A SECURITY SYSTEM, CONSIDER ADDING SCREENS THAT SOUND AN ALARM WHEN CUT

JOIN A NEIGHBORHOOD WATCH GROUP

LOCK ALL YOUR DOORS AND WINDOWS

Even though a locked door or window may not stop a determined intruder, the noise created by his breaking a lock or the sound of a window breaking will give you warning so you can call 911 and prepare for what's happening.

If, despite your precautionary actions, an intruder enters your home, the time to choose an action plan is now, before that scary time comes. Just as you have prepared yourself and your children for dealing with a fire in your home, prepare for the possibility that you may have an intruder. When you prepare for the possibility of a fire, you remember simple rules for when the smoke alarm goes off. If you are in your bedroom and the door feels hot, don't open it. If smoke is coming under the door, don't go out there. The escape plan may be to open the bedroom window and crawl outside or jump onto the lawn below. These actions are unpleasant to think about, but you have a plan, and your loved ones know what to do.

Do the same thing for a night intruder. Have a plan so everyone knows what to do.

There are three general plans for dealing with an intruder. Choice 1 is victim behavior. Choice 2 is mildly proactive. Choice 3 is "Not me!" behavior.

CHOICE 1. **HIDE-AND-HOPE.** Using this strategy, you get under the bed, go into the closet, or get out of sight, hoping that the intruder just wants your stuff. If the intruder is just a thief and doesn't find you while he's stealing, this strategy can work. If, however, he is there because he wants to hurt you, or if he finds you while he is stealing and sees an opportunity to hurt you as well as steal, then the hide-and-hope strategy is not effective. Hide-and-hope is victim behavior because it gives too much control to the attacker.

CHOICE 2. **ESCAPE.** Using this strategy, you intend to get out of the house, hoping the intruder does not catch you or chase you. If you or your children have bedrooms on the first floor, this strategy can work. If your bedrooms are on the second or third stories, this strategy is dangerous. Though choosing Escape is more proactive than Hide-and-Hope, it still gives the intruder control and forces you to simply react.

CHOICE 3. **PREPARE-AND-RESIST.** This is the "Not me!" strategy. Prepare by having a family meeting where you discuss what the family will do if an intruder comes to your home. If anyone hears an intruder breaking a window or door lock, everyone immedi-

gun safe in headboard or drawer

ately goes to the safe room. The safe room is predetermined to be the room best equipped to deal with an intruder. This room may have the best escape possibilities or the best floor plan to create space between the intruder and homeowners. The safe room may the one room with a lock on it, a phone, or the room with space behind the clothes in the closet that isn't easy to see by someone unfamiliar with the house. If children sleep on a different floor, they lock their bedroom door or go to a safe room with a door lock, such as the bathroom, and lock the door until Mom or Dad come to get them. As soon as the children have gone to the safe room, they call 911 for help. This is all the children need to know. They do not need to know what follows below.

What the parents know is that in their bedroom are three things: phone, pistol, and tac light (tactical light—that's a fancy name for a flashlight that has an activating switch on its end rather than on its side). The pistol and tac light are safely stored in a small gun safe near the bed. Once the children are in the master bedroom, everyone gets together behind some cover, such as a bed. One of you calls 911 to get help while the other holds the pistol and the tac light.

If the intruder is just taking things and is not coming near the bedroom, everyone stays quiet except for the person talking in a low voice to the 911 operator. If the intruder starts coming upstairs or down the hall to the bedroom, then the person with the pistol and the light yells, "Get out of here! We are talking with 911, and the police are coming right now! Don't come in here!" Hopefully the intruder will become scared and leave. But if he is drunk, on drugs, or has been stalking you, he may continue coming toward your bedroom. You must decide what to do when you see him in the doorway. To help your decision, remember that:

HE BROKE INTO YOUR HOME
He has no regard for the law or the sanctity of your home.

HE HAD AN OPPORTUNITY TO JUST TAKE STUFF AND LEAVE
He is doing more than that; he apparently wants contact with you.

HE IGNORED YOUR WARNINGS AND IS COMING INTO YOUR BEDROOM
This is the most private place in your home, and he is invading it.

Law enforcement people have seen what happens to people when bad guys capture them in the isolation of their homes. The bad guys frequently separate and isolate the family members, rape/torture/abuse them individually, and then kill them so no witnesses survive.

In most states, the practical standard that dictates when you are justified using deadly force (a gun) is linked to whether or not a reasonable person would conclude that the intruder is about to commit a felony against a person. If a reasonable person would conclude that the intruder is about to assault a person in their home, then deadly force is justified. If you have done what is outlined above, a reasonable person knows that this person has broken into your home, ignored your instructions to get out of your house, and ignored your warnings that the police are coming. Now the intruder is coming into your bedroom.

GIVEN THIS SCENARIO, DEADLY FORCE IS PROBABLY JUSTIFIABLE.

You must decide what is right for you and your family. In our house, whoever has the tac light and pistol will illuminate the intruder as he comes through our bedroom doorway. It will be clear in an instant whether we know the person or not. If the person is someone we know and is drunk or under chemical influence and appears to be in our home by mistake, we will use restraint. If the person is someone we don't know, the intruder will be shot rather than allowed to enter our bedroom. If the intruder is shot, we will remain behind cover until the police arrive, because the intruder may have an accomplice and we don't want to become vulnerable to an attack by the accomplice while we are engaged with the first intruder.

When the police arrive, they will know what has been happening because of their contact with 911. 911 will tell you when the police have arrived at your home. Before the police get to your bedroom, put the pistol on the bed in front of you and hold your empty hands up to show police that you do not have a pistol. Then have your meltdown and let the police handle the situation.

If you use the Prepare-and-Resist strategy, you will have protected yourself and your loved ones. All your children have to know is:

- If you hear something that sounds like an intruder, come to our bedroom and tell us. If you hear us yell, "Intruder," come to our bedroom (or go to your safe room and lock the door).

- Then we'll call 911 and get help.

They don't need to know about other portions of the plan that may scare them.

So these are your three choices. Prepare-and-Resist is the most proactive. Escape is the intermediate choice. Hide-and-Hope is the most victim-like. If you are not comfortable with Prepare-and-Resist, then select Escape or Hide-and-Hope. But please don't live in denial. Any plan is better than no plan. Pick your plan and have your family meeting so everyone knows what to do if something bad happens.

Prepare

MAKE YOUR HOME APPEAR TO BE A HARD TARGET COMPARED TO OTHERS. KNOW WHAT YOUR PLAN IS IF YOU HAVE A NIGHT INTRUDER—BEFORE YOU HAVE ONE.

chapter 9

Visualize
WINNING

chapter 9
Visualize
Winning

L et's make all this real for you.

Go back to your heron and frog nightmare scenario—the one that scares you the most. Visualize it.

Now think about one or two things you can do to not be in this scenario. At the top of your list should be "listen to my Creep Meter" and GET AWAY if anything feels wrong or weird. Put the book down for a moment and think about what else you can do to prevent or avoid being in this situation.

ITEMS ON YOUR LIST COULD INCLUDE:

- Plan ahead and be with a friend.

- Have a weapon in your purse or pocket to deter an attacker.

- Be near lights.

- Be near people (mixed couples, husband/wife combinations, or families are best).

- Pick a safer time to be there (during daylight hours).

- If you're in your car, keep driving if something doesn't feel right.

- Avoid isolated areas.

- Plan ahead to avoid this situation.

- Take away any distractions (phone, radio, ear buds, packages, etc.).

- Walk with intention.

- Manage your personal space.

- Make strong eye contact.

Be creative. Stay at this step until you have at least two actions you can take to not be in this situation.

Now imagine your nightmare assailant approaching you in the scenario. Imagine trying to get away, but he has you trapped and is approaching you. See two or three actions you can take to cause him surprise and overwhelming pain so you can escape. At the top of the list is the Cat Move. If his face gets in front of you, do the Cat Move first and fast—he can't protect himself. Pause for a moment, put the book down, and select one or two other items from your bag of tricks.

OTHER OPTIONS INCLUDE:

- Side Cat Move

- Overarm Cat Move

- Bicep curl

- Rag doll

- Scream

- Prepare to use a weapon

- Bite his Adam's apple, tongue, unit, or finger

- Use "give a little to get a lot" to set him up for any of the tricks above

Pick your favorite trick for the situation you're in. Imagine surprising him and doing it with commitment. See him reacting with surprise and overwhelming pain. Now see yourself getting away. Experience the details of your escape. Make it totally real in your vision.

Now quickly run through the scenario again, so the prevention tools and escape tricks become familiar and you don't have to pause to think of them.

Congratulations! You faced your nightmare scenario and your nightmare attacker. You used what you learned to prevent or avoid the situation and escape if the worst happens. You won!

If you are ever facing a situation that scares you, do this exercise again. Pull your car over in a safe location and stop. Sit down for a moment. Pause and lean against a wall. Visualize how you are going to be safer. Take a moment to create your plan to prevent or avoid being in danger. Then remember your favorite escape tricks if, somehow, the worst happens. Now you are prepared to be safer.

SUMMARY

Here is a recap of the most important points about prevention, avoidance, and escape. These three actions are the keys to being safer. Use them; they will not fail you.

1. ***Creep Meter.*** We all have it. It will tell you when something isn't right. If it is sending any signals, GET AWAY!

2. ***Cat Move.*** If you can't get away, go for the Cat Move. Go first and fast. You will cause him so much pain that he will be immobilized and you can escape.

3. ***Never give up.*** You have a bag of tricks that attackers aren't prepared for. If you refuse to give up and are a little patient, one of your tricks will suit the situation and you can escape.

Emotional Healing After
a **BAD THING** Happens

chapter 10
Emotional Healing After a Bad Thing Happens

Bad things happen, even to good people. Each of us has to figure out our own answer to "Why?"

As I see it, everything about our existence relates to learning and growing. Whether it's about learning to walk and move, learning subjects in school, learning about relationships and love, learning about how society functions, or learning about cruelty and pain, these are about growth. If something bad has happened, the greatest challenge and opportunity is to take that negative experience and turn it into something positive by growing from it.

As we explore healing, be aware of two simple facts:

1. ***Healing involves many parties.*** When an assault happens, the victim's healing process will

include feelings about the attacker, those who were involved but were not the attacker, friends involved in the aftermath, family involved in the aftermath, counselors/therapists who are involved, intimate partners who are aware of what happened and react to it, law enforcement personnel who may have been involved, your community of acquaintances who react to the event, and any other people linked to the event.

2. ***The healing process is not linear.*** It involves progress, regression, and progress again. It is often two steps forward and one step back. And this forward/back process may happen with each of the parties linked to the event.

Though healing is a complicated topic, there are common threads in models of healing. In the course of teaching our classes, seeing successful healing happen, and exploring this topic with professionals, I have come to this model of healing. There are many other models that are more sophisticated; mine is simplified so it can be offered in the context of this book.

Think of emotional space as that part of your consciousness that is filled by feelings. That space is never empty—we always have feelings. The process of emotional healing involves feelings of denial, anger, depression, and integration.

STEP 1: DENIAL

Immediately after the event, victims go numb. It's often too painful to fully acknowledge what happened. Questions pile up about how it could have occurred. They try to figure out how to get through the next minutes, hours, and days. Then, gradually, they admit to themselves the realities of what happened. Acknowledgment happens in layers, at a pace they can deal with. Accepting that it happened is painful and difficult. Accepting that it happened is also very important, because it is the first step in the healing process. The healing process will get stuck until denial ends and acceptance occurs.

We are as sick as our secrets. If we suppress acceptance, we create a problem. Think of the secret as a capsule filled with negative energy. It will exist until the negative energy is dissipated. Sooner or later the capsule will leak and its contents will result in physical, emotional, psychological, or relationship dysfunctions. The only way to prevent that from happening is to move through denial by accepting that the bad thing happened and sharing it with others so healing energy can neutralize the negative energy. Share it to heal it. Those who care about the victim will provide healing love, compassion, and support.

The ER is part of the first step. If the worst happens, get the victim to the emergency room at a large hospital. Most large hospitals have SAFE (Sexual Assault Forensic Examiner) or SANE (Sexual Assault Nurse Examiner) nurses on 30-minute call 24/7/365. These trained specialists will treat physical issues that need attention and correlate physical evidence to the victim's story so it can be used in prosecution of an attacker if that happens. Many states protect victims, and law enforcement is not called in unless the victim requests their involvement. Regardless of whether police are involved or not, the nurse will help.

There are times when a victim can't bring herself to go to the hospital immediately following the assault. That's understandable. Even if there is a delay, go to the hospital. Medical issues can be handled. Bruises will be evident, and DNA may be recoverable even after four to five days. There is another important reason to go. Telling the story to the nurse requires accepting that it happened, and relating it in detail to the nurse makes telling the story to others much easier.

STEP 2: ANGER

After accepting that it happened and sharing it, emotions shift to anger. Victims feel anger toward the attacker, toward anyone who helped the event happen, toward those who didn't react appropriately, and toward anyone who hurt their feelings in the aftermath. Many situations, many feelings, much anger. Normal. That anger gives victims something to focus on or attach to. It's part of the process. Letting yourself get mad, as fully mad as you can, and blowing it all out is the best way to get rid of anger and move through the process. Screaming, kicking, and punching pillows work well so long as you aren't hurting yourself or others. And you may have to go through venting anger toward several parties related to the event, so this step may take a while.

STEP 3: DEPRESSION

After anger comes depression from the feeling of great loss. The world we want to live in just isn't the same. Trust has been breached, boundaries have been broken, and the world doesn't feel safe anymore. The victim feels vulnerable, hopeless, guilty, shameful, or fearful. Depression is a natural and normal part of the healing process. To one degree or another, everyone goes through depression as part of healing. Just as with anger, let it happen.

As the questions come, begin answering them in positive ways. "Can I still trust people?" Yes, most people can be trusted, but some can't. "Is my world safe?" Yes, most places are safe, but some aren't. Ask your questions and shape positive answers. While you are doing that, do activities that bring you joy, such as being outdoors, holding a pet, or expressing yourself creatively. As with the other steps, victims may have to go through depression more than once as they deal with various parties related to the event.

Emotional Healing After
a Bad Thing Happens

STEP 1 DENIAL
It's often too painful to fully acknowledge what happened.

STEP 2 ANGER
After accepting that it happened and sharing it, emotions shift to anger.

STEP 3 DEPRESSION
After anger comes depression from the feeling of great loss.

STEP 4: INTEGRATION

The final step of healing is integration. As the victim experiences all the feelings, asks and answers all the questions, and merges all that into daily life, the healing process becomes complete. The victim does not return to their pre-assault state. All the feelings and experiences related to the event will have merged into another dimension of the victim. The lessons learned will help prepare them for the future. By integrating the lessons and incorporating all the positive energy others contributed along the way, there can be growth.

Final

Thought

chapter 11
Final
Thought

Affirmations spoken out loud are powerful tools. Positive affirmations strengthen and enable us.

Please say the following affirmation aloud, "I am not a victim. Not me." The more empowered you feel, the easier that is to say.

Now say it three more times aloud.

"I AM NOT A VICTIM. **NOT ME!**"
"I AM NOT A VICTIM. **NOT ME!**"
"I AM NOT A VICTIM. **NOT ME!**"

Each time you say this affirmation, you will feel a little more empowered—a little stronger. When you have said it enough times, you will feel ready for action if necessary.

As you read these last sentences, slow down. Take a couple deep breaths. Consider your life—what you do each day. Parts of your life are low risk, such as when you are in your safe place. But when you leave your safe place, risk increases. Some places and activities are high risk. When you are in your safe place, turn off your Creep Meter and be at peace. We all need time to balance ourselves. But as soon as you leave your safe place, become aware of those around you.

Most people are like you, filling their day with all the activities required by life and doing good things. But when your day's travels bring you into contact with someone who feels compelled to hurt others, you can prevent becoming part of the scene by trusting your feelings—and getting away immediately. If, however, you find yourself trapped and can't get away, you can escape using courage and the information in this book.

As you consider your life, see the joy and beauty in it. Enjoy your life. And know that you are now safer.

THE BEGINNING
OF YOUR SAFER LIFE

PREPARATION WHEN YOU TRAVEL:

Dress simply with no flashy jewelry that draws attention.

AT THE AIRPORT
- Arrange to be dropped off and picked up by someone you know.

- If you have to park, get close to an elevator or use valet service.

- If you have to walk any significant distance, get a security guard escort.

- On the airplane, don't give strangers information about where you are staying; don't let them see your itinerary and accommodations information.

WHEN YOU ARRIVE AT YOUR DESTINATION AIRPORT
- Have someone you know pick you up if possible.

- If you take a cab, do the following:

  - use cabs from the starter, no freelancers.

  - make certain that the picture on the cab permit matches the face of your driver.

  - Know the route to your destination using MapQuest or equivalent.

  - Have instructions written in the local language.

AT YOUR HOTEL
- Request a "women only" floor if the hotel has one.

- Get a room near the elevator so you don't have to wander long halls.

- If someone is threatening you, yell, "Fire!" to get more attention than "Help!"

- Check to make certain your room is safe before you deadbolt the door.

- Guard your room number so strangers can't determine where you are staying.

- Let no one into your room except uniformed room service people delivering items you ordered.

GETTING AROUND

- Get rides from people you know as much as possible.

- Use cabs from the hotel's starter rather than freelancers.

- Know where you are going and know the best route.

- Get written directions in the local language.

- Do not get out of the cab until you are at your destination; close is not good enough.

IF YOU GET INTO TROUBLE

- Know whom you are going to call if you get into trouble.

- Know if the local police are trustworthy.

- Know the number for the U.S. Consulate or other friendly resource if local officials are not trustworthy.

- If something feels wrong, get away immediately.

PREPARATION AROUND HOME:

- Make your house appear to be a "hard target" by showing "Beware of dog" and "Security System" signs.

- Put up motion-activated lights by the front and back entrances.

- Replace or re-key locks when you move into a new home or apartment.

- Install good quality deadbolt door locks.

- Lock doors and windows—forcing intruders to make noise on the way in.

- Have a family meeting and agree on your intruder strategy— Hide-and-Hope, Escape, or Prepare-and-Resist.

- Open your door only for people you know and trust. Only let service or repair people in whom you have scheduled in advance.

- If you come home and see anything unusual, find someone you trust to enter the house with you or call 911.

- Do not let someone in to make a phone call—make the call for him.

- If someone enters your home, and anything feels wrong, get away immediately.

PREPARATION AROUND CARS:

- Keep a map in your car to help you if you get lost.
- Lock your doors both when you are in your car and when it is parked.
- Allow only people you trust completely to be in your car with you.
- If you are being followed, drive to a police/fire station or a place where there are bright lights and many people.
- Have your car key detachable from your home key when giving your keys to a parking attendant or valet.
- Do not stop in an unsafe place. Drive to safety on flat tires and with minor damage to your car.
- Look in the backseat before you get into your car.
- If you have car trouble, raise your hood and stay in your locked vehicle. When someone offers help, roll your window down just a little to get help. Stay in your locked car until someone you trust arrives.
- If someone tries to force his way into your car, use the accelerator and escape.
- If an attacker is forcing you to drive to isolation, crash into something solid (tree, telephone pole, etc.) and escape.
- If an attacker is driving you to isolation, try to cause a crash into something solid and escape.
- Carry a cell phone to get help in emergencies.
- If anything feels wrong, get away immediately.

PREPARATION ON THE STREET:

- Walk in groups; not alone.
- Walk around areas that can hide attackers (alleys, bushes).
- Avoid dark areas.

- Walk facing traffic so you can see who is approaching.

- Have car keys, house keys, ATM cards, etc. ready so you minimize time you expose your blind side.

- Carry a weapon of some sort—see chapter 4 on weapons—even if it's just a pen. If someone threatens you, go into your "Not me!" mind-set, show the weapon, make eye contact, and get away.

- If someone or someplace doesn't feel right, get away immediately.

- DO NOT GET TRANSPORTED by an attacker.

PREPARATION FOR PARTYING:

- Go with friends you trust and agree on rules before you go:
  - No one leaves with a stranger.
  - No one who has had too much to drink is left alone.
  - Everyone leaves if someone is drugged.

- Do not get separated from the group with a stranger.

- If you didn't see the drink from the bartender's hand to your hand, don't drink it.

- If you think you have been drugged, get with someone you trust immediately or call 911.

- If someone or someplace doesn't feel right, get away immediately.

IF YOU ARE ASSAULTED:

- Report every attack. It's not your fault!

- Call 911 immediately.

- Do not change clothes or clean up—evidence may be affected.

- Do not use the bathroom (if possible)—evidence may be affected.

- Do not eat, smoke, or chew gum—evidence may be affected.

- Write down everything you can remember while it's fresh in your mind:

    Car make, model, color, license number.

    Race of attacker.

    Age, weight, and height

    Color of hair

    Color of eyes

    Clothing

    Unusual marks, scars, tattoos, rings, etc.

    Facial hair

    Odors

- Once the reporting activities are done, get the support and emotional help you need.

SHARING YOUR VALUABLE KNOWLEDGE...

If you face a dangerous encounter and use the techniques in this book, or other techniques, to win, please consider sharing that valuable experience with other girls and women. Join us online and "Like Us" on Facebook. See what has worked well for other girls and women on this page.

IF YOU ENJOYED THIS BOOK and want to give additional copies to girls and women you care about, visit us at:

www.**NotMeTraining**.com

 @NotMeTraining    NotMeTraining

APPENDIX